Contents

Social Work with Older People

KARIN CRAWFORD AND JANET WALKER

Series Editors: Jonathan Parker and Greta Bradley

LearningMatters

First published in 2004 by Learning Matters Ltd.

British Library Cataloguing in Publication Data
A CIP record for this book is available from the British Library.

ISBN 1 84445 017 1

Cover and text design by Code 5 Design Associates Ltd
Project management by Deer Park Productions
Typeset by Pantek Arts Ltd, Maidstone, Kent
Printed and bound in Great Britain by Bell & Bain Ltd, Glasgow

Learning Matters Ltd
33 Southernhay East
Exeter EX1 1NX
Tel: 01392 215560
info@learningmatters.co.uk
www.learningmatters.co.uk

Introduction

The Quality Assurance Agency for Higher Education sets out the subject benchmarks and academic standards for Social Work. The agency describes social work as *characterised by a distinctive focus on practice in complex social situations to promote and protect individual and collective well-being*. Benchmark statement 5.2.1 states that students should develop the *ability to use knowledge and understanding in work within specific practice contexts*. This book has a distinctive focus on social work practice within the specific practice context of working with older people.

The book has been written for student social workers who are beginning to develop their skills and understanding of the requirements for practice, particularly social work practice with older people. While it is primarily aimed at students in their first and second years or levels of study, it will be potentially useful across your whole programme of study and as you move into relevant areas of practice learning. Your studies through this book will develop your knowledge, skills and values in working with older people, so that you will confidently promote and protect the individual and collective well-being of the older people with whom you work.

The book will also appeal to you if you are considering a career in social work or social care but are not yet studying for a social work degree. It will assist students undertaking a range of social and healthcare courses in further education. Nurses, occupational therapists and other health and social care professionals will be able to gain an insight into the new requirements demanded of social workers. Experienced and qualified social workers, especially those contributing to practice learning, will also be able to use this book for consultation, teaching and revision and to gain an insight into the expectations raised by the qualifying degree in social work.

Requirements for social work education

Social work education has undergone a major transformation to ensure that qualified social workers are educated to honours degree level and develop knowledge, skills and values which are common and shared. A vision for social work operating in complex human situations has been adopted. This is reflected in the following definition from the International Association of Schools of Social Work and International Federation of Social Workers (2001):

The social work profession promotes social change, problem solving in human relationships and the empowerment and liberation of people to enhance well-being. Utilising theories of human behaviour and social systems, social work intervenes at the points where people interact with their environments. Principles of human rights and social justice are fundamental to social work.

Therefore social work concerns individual people and wider society, working with people who are vulnerable and may be struggling in some way to participate fully in society. Social workers work at the interface between the marginalised individual and the social and political environment that may have contributed to their marginalisation. Social workers need to be highly skilled and knowledgeable to work effectively in this context.

In order to improve the quality of professional social work, it is crucial that you, as a student social worker, develop a rigorous grounding in and understanding of theories and models for social work. Such knowledge helps social workers to know what to do, when to do it and how to do it, while recognising that social work is a complex activity with no absolute 'rights' and 'wrongs' of practice for each situation.

Throughout the book, connections are made to the relevant key elements of the prescribed National Curriculum, the Quality Assurance Agency academic benchmark criteria for social work and the National Occupational Standards for social work. The five core areas of knowledge, as identified for social work students by the Department of Health, are integrated within the chapters of the book as follows:

- *Human growth and development*. The life course perspective of growth and development in older adulthood is addressed throughout the book but most specifically within Chapters 1 and 2.

- *Assessment, planning, intervention and review*. The processes of social work practice with older people are most evident in the activities and discussion within Chapters 3, 4, 5, 6 and 7.

- *Law for social workers*. The legal context of social work practice with older people is a core element of Chapter 3. Additionally, Chapters 6 and 7 make a more in-depth exploration of two key national strategies.

- *Communicating with people*. The importance of effective communication with older people is, again, integral throughout the book. However, specific skills and knowledge necessary to facilitate effective communication with older adults who experience needs related to mental disorder, learning disability, physical disability and/or sensory impairments is particularly pertinent within Chapters 4 and 5. Within Chapter 6 you will consider the specific skills of communicating with older people who may be vulnerable, at risk of or experiencing abusive situations. The final chapter of the book, Chapter 7, addresses communication skills necessary to develop and maintain effective working partnerships with older people and other agencies.

- *Working interprofessionally*. Chapter 7 of the book is dedicated to exploring interprofessional working as a key element within the concepts of partnership and participation with others. Additionally Chapter 6 develops a strong emphasis on working together across disciplines and agencies, the sharing of information and joint decision-making.

In essence, the book concentrates on perspectives on practice with older people that are current in practice and transferable across settings. An action-oriented approach helps to facilitate your developing understanding, evaluation and review of your practice. Case studies, activities and summaries of contemporary research will be used to illustrate and draw out key points, to aid and reinforce your learning. You will also be provided with suggestions for further reading, Internet resources and current government guidance and policy documents, all of which evidence and support best social work practice when working with older people.

Book structure

As will be seen from the chapter outlines below, the book starts by taking a broad approach to social work practice with older people as it considers in the early chapters the context of this particular area of practice. This is then used as the basis for the later chapters, which take a more detailed look at specific areas of practice. The emphasis in this book concerns you achieving the requirements of the curriculum and developing knowledge that will assist you in meeting the Occupational Standards for social work.

Chapter 1 addresses the social work benchmark statement 5.2.2 – subject skills – which requires social work graduates to have an understanding of ethical issues and codes of values and practice in specific situations. It also makes explicit links to the GSCC Code of Practice for employees and the GSCC Code of Practice for employers. The chapter addresses the ways in which values and ethics apply in social work practice with older people through an examination of the issues of ageism, inequality and oppression. You will be encouraged to examine your own concepts of later life, your values, prejudices and the implications for practice. Social differences that affect the position of older people in society, for example social class, gender and ethnic differences, and the links to problems of inequality and differential need faced by older people are explored throughout the chapter. You will consider how social processes can lead to marginalisation, isolation and exclusion of older people and can impact on the demand for social work services. With particular reference to concepts such as prejudice, interpersonal, institutional and structural discrimination, empowerment and anti-discriminatory practices, you will develop your understanding about the nature of social work services and social work practice in a diverse society.

By developing the discussion about the position of older people in society from Chapter 1, the second chapter considers how the cultural, economic and social context of being an older person impacts upon and influences social work practice and services with older people. Thus Chapter 2 is about the context of social work practice with older people. Through the use of activities and follow-up comments that focus on the implications for social work practice with older service users, the chapter encourages you to examine how service delivery and practice might be influenced by the way in which ageing is conceptualised in our society. The chapter locates contemporary social work practice with older people within both historical and comparative perspectives, including European and international contexts.

In Chapter 3 you will examine the significance of legislative and legal frameworks, policy directives and service delivery standards on social work practice with older people. The social work subject benchmark 3.1.2 describes the knowledge, understanding and skills required in a service delivery context, particularly the significance of legislative and legal frameworks and service delivery standards. The complex relationships between public, social and political philosophies, policies and priorities, and the organisation and practice of social work are integral to the discussions in this chapter. The chapter develops one case study with related activities so that as you work through key areas of legislation and guidance you will be able to draw out the implications for service delivery and practice and for service-users. The main body of the chapter reflects the themes of the government's modernisation agenda and through those themes you will look at key influential national documents and strategies which will include: the National Health Service and Community Care Act 1990, Community Care Direct Payments legislation and guidance, the National Service Framework for Older People, legislation and guidance to support carers of older people, the Care Standards Act 2000, the National Health Service Plan 2000, guidance on the development of eligibility criteria and consideration of ways in which older people have been able to influence the developing legal and political agendas.

Chapters 4 and 5 explore theories, methods and skills required for social work practice with older people who experience specific needs. In these chapters you will consider how these needs are defined and how the social work processes of assessment, planning, intervention and review can take account of the specific experiences and needs of older people. Chapter 4 examines specific issues and needs related to mental disorder and learning disabilities, while Chapter 5 follows the same standards and structure by exploring theories, methods and skills required for social work practice with older people who experience needs related to sensory impairments and physical impairments. Through both of these chapters you will have the opportunity to explore definitions, theoretical explanations and characteristics related to social work practice in these particular contexts.

The focus of Chapter 6 is the concepts of vulnerability, abuse, risks and rights in relation to social work practice with older people. The chapter is particularly relevant to the National Occupational Standards Key Role 4, Unit 12: *Manage risk to individuals, families, carers, groups and communities* and will enable you to consider direct social work practice in respect of the identification, investigation and prevention of abuse alongside meaningful incorporation of the service-user's perspective. You will firstly learn about the historical context of vulnerability and abuse in respect of older adults, particularly focusing on how different terms and definitions have developed and are used in contemporary social work practice. Chapter 6 makes links to Chapter 3 of the book, in that you will think about the legal and political context of working with vulnerable older people, as the chapter is structured around and concentrates on the national policy document on Protection for Vulnerable Adults, *No Secrets: Guidance on Developing and Implementing Multi-agency Policies and Procedures to Protect Vulnerable Adults from Abuse*.

The final chapter of the book, Chapter 7, will enable you to develop your knowledge and skills in the area of partnership working, so that your social work practice with older people ensures the meaningful participation of all stakeholders. The National Service Framework for Older People, Standard Two: *Single Assessment Process*, is taken as an example through which to explore the concepts of partnership and participation in practice. The social work subject benchmark 3.2.4 describes the necessary skills in working with others in social work practice. This will be achieved through Chapter 7 as you look at issues of partnership, participation and working across professional boundaries at different levels. Firstly you will learn about partnership at a structural and strategic level, then at the level of teamworking through the development of networks, systems and skills that are required to maintain effective professional working relationships. The final section of the chapter encourages you to look at ways in which older people who use social work services, their families and carers, can be enabled to participate in services in ways that will increase their resources, capacity and power to influence factors that affect their lives.

The conclusion of the book summarises aspects of learning from within all of the chapters. You will be encouraged to reflect upon, chart and monitor your learning, taking developmental needs and reflections forward through your own ongoing professional development. Specific factors relevant to social work practice with older people are reviewed, particularly the influence of social constructions and disadvantage and how best social work practice can empower and enable older people in their lives.

Learning features

The book is interactive. You are encouraged to work through the text as an active participant, taking responsibility for your learning in order to increase your knowledge, understanding and ability to apply this learning to your practice with older people. You are expected to reflect creatively on how your immediate learning and analysis can impact upon your professional work with older people.

Case studies and activities throughout the book aim to help you to examine concepts, theories and models for social work practice. We have devised activities that require you to reflect on experiences, situations and events and help you to review and summarise learning undertaken. In this way your knowledge will become deeply embedded as part of your development. When you come to undertake social work practice with older people the work and reflection undertaken here will help you to improve and hone your skills and knowledge. Additionally, suggestions for further reading and research are made at the end of each chapter.

Professional development and reflective practice

The importance of professional development is clearly shown by its inclusion in the National Occupational Standards and in the General Social Care Council (GSCC) Code of Practice for Employees. In this book, great emphasis is placed on developing skills of reflection about, in and on practice. It is important that you reflect prior to practice as well as during and after practice situations. The notion of reflective practice has developed over many years in social work. This book will assist you in developing a questioning approach that looks in a critical and analytical way at your thoughts, experiences and practice with older people, as it seeks to heighten your skills in refining your practice as a result of these deliberations. Reflection is central to good social work practice, but only if action results from that reflection.

Reflecting about, in and on your practice is not only important during your education to become a social worker – it is considered key to continued professional development. This approach will draw on and rely on you to acquire high-quality communication skills, skills in working with others, and reflective skills in personal and professional development. Continuing professional development requires you to ensure that research informs your practice and that you are constantly developing your skills and values for practice. It is therefore important that you begin this process at the outset of your learning.

Chapter 1
Values and ethics in social work with older people

Introduction

This chapter will examine issues of ageism, in particular the concepts of discrimination and oppression. You will be encouraged to identify your assumptions and values, in particular examining your own concepts of later life. You will consider and reflect on the theme of prejudice and oppression and the implications for practice with older people.

The chapter explores issues of values and ethics in working with older people. It will examine the social differences that affect the position of older people in society, in particular exploring the issues of social class, gender and ethnic differences. This will be linked to problems of inequality and differential need faced by older people. You will then consider how these social processes can lead to marginalisation, isolation and exclusion and their impact on social work will be considered. This will lead to a discussion about the nature of social work services in a diverse society (with particular reference to concepts such as prejudice, interpersonal, institutional and structural discrimination, empowerment and anti-discriminatory practices).

Developing an understanding of your own starting point

In order to explore the themes of ageism and their impact on your work with older people, it is important that you have an understanding of your own views in relation to older people, both personally and professionally. Try and take an honest approach to your thoughts, attitudes and feelings.

ACTIVITY **1.1**

Think about your views and assumptions about older people. Make a list of words or phrases that describe them. How do you come to hold these beliefs – to know what you know and why they may have taken this direction as opposed to others?

Your answer will, of course, be very personal to you. As a child you may remember thinking that all adults were 'old', especially your parents or other people's parents. As you get older you realise that making distinctions on the basis of age is not as simple as when you were a child: individuals are a lot more diverse, with age being only one factor that makes up the identity of that individual. The contacts and experiences that you have had with older people may have impacted on your views. Other factors such as your family's attitudes, beliefs and cultural background, the beliefs of others such as friends, the religion in which you were brought up, the influence of the media, all will have influenced your views and assumptions on 'older people' and the values and attitudes that you hold.

ACTIVITY 1.2

How do you think that society views older people? What barriers and opportuni_____ in society for older people?

You may have come up with a number of ideas of ways in which society views older people – for example, as those with wisdom and experience that can support and nurture the following generations. Alternatively, the other end of the continuum is that society may view older people as a burden, a drain on resources. Holding this range of attitudes and beliefs will influence the way in which society constructs barriers and opportunities. For example, as people get older they may experience difficulties in getting a job because they are perceived as being at the end of their working lives as opposed to having a positive contribution to make, e.g. in terms of experience. It may be useful for you to share your responses to these two exercises with a fellow student or colleague to discuss similarities and differences. The starting point for thinking about values has to be your own personal perspective. It is important that you examine and continue to re-examine and explore your assumptions, values and attitudes, in this case of older people, on a regular basis.

On a personal level values refer to the beliefs and attitudes that individuals hold. A range of factors may influence these; for example your experience of family life may find you 'upholding' or 'denying' a particular way of thinking or acting because of the influence of your experience within your family or other forms of care you experienced as a child. An example may be that of your experience as a child of older people, for example of your grandparents. What, if any, was your grandparents' involvement in your childhood? Do you view this involvement or non-involvement as a positive or negative experience? As a result of this experience what role do you think that grandparents should have in the lives of their grandchildren? What role do you think that grandchildren should have in the lives of their grandparents? Why? Values may also be influenced by social, moral, religious or political ideology. For example, you may have had a lot of contact with your grandparents when you were a child. Your personal experience may be that this was a positive experience. You may have been further influenced by, for example, the wider views of the importance of family and family networks and the duty of families to care for their older relatives. This may be part of your cultural beliefs and your religious beliefs. It is important that you recognise and challenge your personal beliefs as these may/will have a profound influence on your professional value base.

ACTIVITY 1.3

Think about the opportunities and challenges in working with older people as a social worker. What do you see as the positive benefits of working with older people? What do you see as some of the challenges of working with older people?

You may have a clear view of what working with older people means to you; this may be an area of social work practice that you will choose to work in. Alternatively you may have had little contact with older people; you may feel that your strengths lie in working with children. Of course your views may be anywhere else along this continuum! The following cases are intended to support you in exploring your values and attitudes in relation to older people, particularly situations and their consequent dilemmas that you may experience in social work practice.

ACTIVITY 1.4

Think about the following cases. How do you feel about each of the situations? Can you identify why you feel as you do? What are the beliefs that underpin your thinking? What do you think you should do next? Why?

Malik, age 78, is frightened to leave the house at night. He says that there are too many young people on the street and when he comes out they call him racist names and throw things at him.

Donald, age 89, has recently moved into a home for older people. His mobility is restricted and he is beginning to experience memory impairment and is sometimes confused. When he receives his post he finds that it has been opened and read. He is distressed and angry. Staff says this is normal practice, particularly for people with memory impairment; they may miss important information contained in their post.

Jim is 68 and has dementia. Kay, 62, his wife, cares for him at home but is finding this increasingly difficult. When she tries to tend to his basic needs, such as toileting and bathing him, Jim is often verbally aggressive. He has also been physically aggressive, punching her in the arm and face. Kay feels alienated and frightened; she cannot reconcile Jim as he is now to the professional solicitor and active family man that he was. She finds that she can control Jim if she strikes him with a walking stick.

Gilly, 86, is very independent. She is physically able and spends her day walking around the town pushing an old pram. She searches through dustbins, waste bins and skips, taking anything that she finds interesting. She stores this in her house and garden. Gilly never throws anything away, so the room is piled high with newspapers, books and things that she keeps. The neighbours are complaining about the smell. Her general practitioner expresses a growing concern for her safety.

Malik's experience is clearly very distressing for him. You will need to gain a greater understanding of Malik's situation and his perspective to support you in seeking individual solutions to his experience. However, there are wider community issues here. What is the reason for 'so many young people on the streets'? What may be the reasons behind the racist comments? In seeking to understand this you will need to gain a wider understanding of community issues. Talking to other professionals working in the community will help – the police, schools, youth services, voluntary and community groups. Working together you can consider what could be done to help Malik's individual situation, for example support from the community police officer by visiting Malik to seek an individual solution, and the wider situation, for example support from schools in tackling racism through their curriculum.

In the case of Donald the approach for the home may be 'well meaning'. The assumption would appear to be that people who may be confused are incapable of expressing their views. The damaging effect of this is that it denies people their rights and opportunities to make choices for themselves. The staff's approach could also be seen as intrusive and disrespectful. Donald should be consulted as to what he wants, in this case in relation to his post.

In the case of Jim and Kay who do you perceive as the person in need of help? There are adult protection issues. Jim's treatment of his wife is unacceptable; the fact that he has dementia may be the reason behind this. The strain and pressure of caring for Jim, as well as coming to terms for her loss of *the partner she remembers*, may explain Kay's behaviour. It does not excuse it. An understanding will need to be gained of each of their situations and their perspective on it. You and other professionals involved will need to undertake an assessment of risk and consider how to protect and support Jim in particular. Both will need support and help in coming to terms with their situation.

One of the dilemmas that Gilly presents to us is the issue of her individual rights, including the right to self-determination, and those of her neighbours and community. This may also present you with dilemmas for your professional value base – is Gilly's position unsafe, untenable, unacceptable? In Gilly's case, what constitutes 'safe' or 'safe enough'? What constitutes 'dangerous'? Assessment of her needs will be core to this analysis. Gilly's perception of her needs and the situation in which she lives is essential. You will need to gain the view of others; for example, what is the general practitioner's concern based on – is it Gilly's physical, social and/or emotional need? In any situation such as Donald and Kay, and Gilly, you will need to use your professional judgment – this judgment may be in direct contrast to the views of others, for example neighbours, and other professionals such as the general practitioner.

Understanding and reviewing your personal and professional base and reflecting on the impact of this on your practice are a critical part of your analysis and evaluation, for example in 'transforming' your practice. Using formal supervision, keeping a reflective diary and taking time to think about and reflect on your approach are some of the essential parts of this process.

Ethics and values and their impact on working with older people

What does the word 'ethics' mean in the context of social care practice with older people? In relation to this book we have taken it to mean:

> … the norms or standards of behaviour people follow concerning what is regarded as good or bad, right or wrong. (Banks, 2001: 4)

This may be apparent in the way that social workers work with individuals in ensuring and promoting their right to make decisions and choices. It may be apparent in how social workers respond to the collective needs of groups of people, such as those who are older. It might be apparent in the way that social workers challenge the views and opinions of society, for example in challenging discrimination and oppression in relation to older people. These inevitably can create dilemmas and conflict between the rights of an individual and the wider responsibility of social workers to society.

What does the word 'values' mean in the context of social care with older people? A dictionary definition is that values are 'a principle, standard, or quality considered worthwhile or desirable. One's principles or standards, one's judgment of what is valuable or important in life' (**www.dictionary.com**). Banks (2001) suggests that they are '... a set of fundamental moral/ethical principles to which social workers should be committed' (p 6). Values help to define social work practice, including the parameters and boundaries of practice and behaviour. They help us to make sense of and judge our practice. However, they can challenge our thinking and approach, leading to ambiguity and uncertainty about roles, responsibility and practice.

Values in our practice are guided by professional codes. The National Occupational Standards for Social Work (**www.topss.org.uk**) outline the standards for working with individuals, families, carers, groups and communities to achieve change and development and to promote and enhance life opportunities. These standards are underpinned by values and ethics that must support the development and delivery of your practice. These include practice that demonstrates respect for the individual, maintaining trust and confidentiality, and understanding and making use of strategies to challenge discrimination, disadvantage and other forms of inequality and injustice. These standards are integral to the teaching and learning on the social work degree programme. If you are studying for this degree you will need to demonstrate your knowledge, understanding and application of these values both academically, for example through assessment events, and professionally, for example within your practice placements. We also refer to those standards linked to the themes and issues we cover at the beginning of each chapter. The 'Codes of practice for social workers and employers', developed by the GSCC, are intended to provide a guide for all those who work in social care, setting out the standards of practice and conduct workers and their employers should meet. They are a critical part of regulating the social care workforce and helping to improve levels of professionalism and public protection. In registering with the General Social Care Council (**www.gscc.org.uk**), you are agreeing to uphold the values of social work.

Principles should guide your behaviour and support you in reflecting on your practice. Biestek (1961) has probably had the most profound influence and he identifies seven principles that should underpin social work practice:

- individualisation;

- non-judgmental attitude;

- acceptance;

- purposeful expression of feelings;

- controlled emotional involvement;

- user self-determination; and

- confidentiality.

The principle of respect for others as self-determining individuals and the dignity of the individual underpin these. You should explore the principles that support social work practice further to seek to gain a greater understanding of the meaning and action that underpin them, including critiques; for example, it is suggested that the principles outlined by Biestek are individualistic and culturally specific as they are based on Western culture (Dominelli, 2002). Dominelli (2002) and Banks (2001) offer a good starting point for you to begin this process.

As a social worker you need to recognise how organisational, political and societal values influence your practice and influence and impact on the lives of people, especially older people and their families.

At an organisational level, there may be a conflict between what the organisation believes (the values underpinning practice within that agency) and their ability and power to uphold these. An example might be in the rules and procedures which agencies develop to support the delivery of service. These have the effect of targeting and rationing services, and this may bring you into conflict with what you believe an individual older person needs and what the agency believes that it can provide from a financial perspective. Another concern has been the increasing bureaucratisation of service delivery (more paperwork and forms), which appears to be more about agency rules and procedures than about responsibility to the older person. These issues are discussed further in Chapter 3.

It is suggested by Howe (2002) that 'In the broadest sense, the purposes of social work are determined by prevailing political values' (page 86). These refer to the political ideology, legislation and policy that guide and subsequently influence our practice, for example availability and access to resources. Political ideology is also determined by political philosophy and rhetoric. This may have a powerful effect on agencies and the individual practice of social workers. For example, the difference between 'individualism' (concern for the individual and their behaviour) and 'collectivism' (the cooperation and interdependence of society) which can support different ways of engaging in practice with service users.

ACTIVITY *1.5*

Consider the following:

> *Joan, age 87, has great difficulty doing her shopping. Her mobility is restricted and because of poor public transport she has to walk to her local shops. She often has nothing to eat as she cannot manage the walk.*

What would be an 'individualism' approach to this issue?

What would be a 'collectivism' approach to this issue?

An individualist response would be to assess Joan's particular situation and try to put in place a plan that would seek to meet her individual needs. In undertaking an assessment the social worker would also be assessing other aspects of Joan's life, consequently it might become apparent that her needs are greater than simply for shopping and there is the potential for Joan to receive other sorts of help and support, consequently improving the quality of her life. A collectivist approach might be to consider Joan's needs in the context of the wider needs of older people in the community. What are the particular needs of all older people in accessing services? How can community services and involvement be improved to ensure they are accessible? For example, what is the potential for voluntary agencies to provide a shopping service for older people? Can pressure be put on the local council in relation to planning and support of the development of local shops? What about the development of accessible, local public transport?

Political ideology has been made explicit for older people in the *National Service Framework for Older People* (Department of Health, 2001a). One of the themes of the National Service Framework (NSF) for Older People is 'respecting the individual ... triggered by a concern about widespread infringement of dignity and unfair discrimination in older people's access to care. The NSF therefore leads with plans to tackle age discrimination and to ensure that older people are treated with respect, according to their individual needs' (page 12). In particular Standard 1 relates to 'Rooting out age discrimination' and Standard 2 relates to 'Person-centred care'.

While the ideology of the NSF for Older People clearly supports an agenda based on sound values and practice in relation to practice with older people, there is a significant difference between political ideology and practice. An example is the expectations within the NSF for Older People that there must be in place systems and processes that support ways of working between professions, such as health and social care, to ensure co-operation and continuity of services for older people. This will be a challenge for individuals and professional groups who have to work together; for example, this may be evident in the different values that underpin the 'social model' and 'individual model'. Within the individual model the 'abnormality' or 'dysfunction' is seen as being located in the individual's body. The social model locates the issues within society, organisations and groups in the barriers, values and attitudes that they demonstrate that may discriminate against an individual or group of people. This will be discussed further in Chapters 4 and 5 of this book. As the practice of social work moves towards new organisational processes and structures that stress multi-agency and inter-agency working that integrates professionals from different agencies, these inevitably bring together individuals and professional groups whose values may be similar or different. When working with others and other professional groups you will need to recognise and value other opinions. At the same time you will need to consider how you may challenge and question assumptions, beliefs and attitudes that others may hold, especially if they appear to impact on the older person. You will need to challenge the stereotypes you may hold about individuals and professional groups. All of this will inevitably challenge your values – the way you understand things and how you demonstrate your personal and professional values in your practice.

> *Different agencies and professions stand for different priorities and values and different concepts of health and welfare, representing the necessary diversity in dynamic advanced societies and of human personality in society ... emphasis on freedom may conflict with the need for community, the need for dependence with the pull to independence, the call for justice and fairness with the plea for mercy and understanding. All these values find expression in the assumptions of different professions and all need to be recognised as essential and to be negotiated.*
> *(Loxley, 1997: 44)*

The views of society (public opinion) have an effect on personal values. Such things as political ideology, religious beliefs and the media influence these. This is prescribed in society 'norms', i.e. the way it is accepted that we should behave and act. Formally these may be written down in laws and policy and procedures. This can be evidenced in the way that society expects social workers to act, for example to protect and preserve the rights of the majority. This can come into conflict with the values of individuality and self-determination.

Defining age

How should we define 'old age'? What are the characteristics and attributes that 'transform' an individual into an older person? How is older age imagined and understood – by you, by those working in social care and by society in general? What impact do these views and opinions have on the way older people are perceived and treated by individuals and society? These are some of the important questions that we are seeking to address within this chapter.

You will now explore the construction of 'age' by thinking about the concepts and ideas that define and label who we are and impact on our perceived position in everyday society.

ACTIVITY **1.6**

Reflect on the following:

What is your chronological age? What expectations and assumptions do others make in relation to your age? Are there any expectations in relation to your age by society? What images are presented on television, in magazines and in newspapers? How have your experiences in the past led and helped you to decide on your current life course, for example your choice to become a social worker? How do you view your future?

Your responses to these questions will of course be influenced by a range of factors related to your personal experience, the expectations of others and the expectations of society. There may an expectation of what you are doing or should have achieved at the age you have reached. For example, if you are a young person of 18 undertaking a degree, this may be viewed as appropriate, 'sensible' and to your advantage in ensuring that you have a better paid job in the future, a career. However, within social work you could be viewed as young and lacking in life experiences. This may be reinforced by the way in which the media portrays your age group through images that show young people as irresponsible and selfish. If you are older, for example if you are in your thirties, you may share a similar experience to this younger person of being viewed as someone seeking to better themselves by undertaking a degree. Or it could be that others may see you as selfish – for example, giving up another career to study for a degree that may put a financial burden on your family. None or all of this may be true! These are all stereotypes – categorising someone or something according to a fixed and rigid set of ideas and principles.

The issue here is that there is a whole range of factors that denote and influence who we are. Age is one of the important factors. We would suggest that 'Age is a social division; it is the dimension of the social structure on the basis of which power, privilege and opportunities tend to be allocated' (Thompson, 2001: 88).

Exploring the concept of ageism

There are a number of definitions of 'ageism'. Butler and Lewis (1973) suggest that 'Ageism can be seen as a process of systematic stereotyping of and discrimination against people because they are old, just as racism and sexism accomplish this for skin colour and gender' (page 30). It is suggested by Bytheway (1995) that 'ageism is prejudice on the grounds of age' (page 9), while Hughes and Mtezuka (1992) describe ageism as 'the social process through which negative images of and attitudes towards older people, based solely on the characteristics of old age itself, result in discrimination' (page 220).

ACTIVITY *1.7*

What are the common 'themes' within these definitions? Do you agree or disagree with any of them? Why?

All these definitions emphasise the negative aspects of 'ageism', reinforcing the fact that they are based on stereotypes and prejudice leading to discrimination. There is some debate among authors, even in these definitions, as to what constitutes ageism. For example, Bytheway (1995) would disagree with the suggestion that ageism is a 'process'. He believes that this is how ageism is made evident – through the behaviour, practices, routines and regulations of everyday practice. He proposes that ageism is an 'ideology' – a set of beliefs that justify the way one group, usually the dominant group, treats another. It would appear that the only common factor to ageism is age itself and that it is usually negative and discriminatory.

Chronological age has a powerful effect on how we are perceived, the expectations of others and the opportunities that may be available to us. Just as young people may be judged as one group because they are teenagers with certain physical and social attributes ascribed to them, so too are older people. But how is it, for example, that we class together in one group people who are sixty years old and people who are ninety years old? Reaching retirement appears to be an important definition to mark reaching older age. This may be perceived as a movement from a previous to a new life. For example, people who are retired are generally expected to have opportunities to take life more leisurely; they are ascribed a particular status because of the words that describe them – aged, retired, pensioners or, more negatively, senile, over the hill. Yet there are many contradictions to this. Traditionally, retirement has been defined as a predictable point when work is expected to stop and is accompanied by a pension, usually provided by the state. Yet the contrast in industrial societies is that this may not come at the traditional stage of the individual's life course; issues of voluntary redundancy, forced and voluntary early retirement, unemployment and so on all have an impact on our detachment from work. The predictability of retirement is being replaced by insecurity and uncertainly about employment in middle and later life.

It would appear that the only common characteristic of this group is that they are 'ordinary people who happen to have reached a particular age' (Tinker, 1996: 6).

In thinking about social work with older people you will have had your own personal experience, assumptions and beliefs. Because of these personal theories and views (concepts) we have particular ideas on how we perceive older people. This will influence your approach and the kind of interventions you make in working with older people. It is through testing these assumptions that we accumulate knowledge and use this to develop and challenge our understanding of the nature of old age, reflecting on the implications for our personal beliefs and our professional practice.

Life course perspectives on later adulthood

Old age is generally stereotyped by physical appearance. Cognitive and social change may follow a different rate of development – a person may look older but continue to retain mental alertness and positive, young, social attitudes.

Taking a biological perspective it can be suggested that most living organisms show an age-related decline: there are changes related to the cells within the body which are usually associated with decline. It is suggested that ageing is universal as it occurs in all members of the population, it is a continuous process and it is intrinsic and degenerative (Bond et al., 1993). This approach proposes that old age is associated with increasing frailty and dependency and there is no possibility for development. However, such changes are not universal and do not affect all individuals in the same way. Other aspects of people's lives impact on individual development such as social, environmental and psychological factors (Crawford and Walker, 2003).

One of the most influential psychosocial approaches to older age has been through the work of Erik Erikson (1995). Erikson states that each stage of life includes a series of dilemmas that the individual needs to achieve a favourable balance before moving on to the next phase. Erikson viewed late adulthood, the final phase of life, as the period of 'integrity versus despair'. This involves accepting a sense of wholeness and ownership of one's life and the choices that were made, without harbouring regret or feelings of having inadequately fulfilled one's life. The goal is the achievement of integrity. Erikson believed that when this is not achieved (despair), then this ultimately leads to a fear of the end of life.

The life course approach suggests that to understand people's experience in later life it is necessary to see them in the context of their life history taking a narrative or biographical approach (Sugarman, 1986). This focuses on the importance of first-hand accounts of people's lives and the meaning they attach to it in influencing and shaping those lives. This approach focuses on the uniqueness of individuals' lives which allows for an exploration of the different aspects of the life course – physical, social, psychological – and that person's unique experience and response to these different aspects. This approach also recognises the interface and influence between the person's individual characteristics and the environment – the psychosocial circumstances: for example, the influence of parents and family, and the impact of wider social issues such as class, race and gender. In taking this approach you are demonstrating the value of that person and that person's individual experience.

The experience of prejudice and discrimination by older people

Prejudice refers to an inflexibility of mind and thought, to values and attitudes that stand in the way of fair and non-judgmental practice. This is linked to real or imagined characteristics of the person, suggesting that they share a propensity to certain sorts of behaviour. Some people may hold explicit ageist views against older people. It is also embedded in social and cultural attitudes and values. This may be demonstrated in the way you talk to a person – resulting in the individual withdrawing from giving you information or conforming, for example, to stereotypes ('sweet old lady', 'good old boy') in order to receive a service. Prejudice is prejudging someone on the basis of their chronological age. Sometimes it is about different generations and the lack of understanding and/or failure to make sense of the differences in life and life experiences. Prejudice in relation to ageism generates and reinforces a fear and denigration of the ageing process, and stereotyping presumptions regarding the competence of the individual, often linked to the need for protection or segregation. Prejudicial attitudes lead to discriminatory practices; this in turn can influence institutional practice and policies. For example, within institutional settings, there may be routines and processes that support the needs of the institution and the staff rather than the needs and wishes of the older people who live there.

ACTIVITY *1.8*

Consider this statement from a manager of a home for older people: 'I was inducting a new member of staff who has recently joined us from another home. When I told her that the people who live in this home could get up in the morning whenever they like, she was shocked! At her previous home breakfast was always served at 7:30 a.m. This meant that staff got some residents out of bed at 5 a.m. so that everyone could be ready for breakfast.

When asked what was the justification, the member of staff was told it as seen as a way in which the night staff "helped" the day staff – residents were clean and ready for breakfast when the day staff came on duty. Also the cook was able to get on with cooking the lunch.'

As a social worker you have been asked to visit this home following a complaint about this issue. How would you challenge this approach?

Caring for people in residential care and ensuring that you meet the needs of all the individuals can be demanding and difficult. It is recognised that routines and processes are inevitable: these even occur in small family groups. However, when they support poor and inappropriate practices, for example appearing to meet the needs of the staff rather than the people whose home it is, then this is totally unacceptable. It may be that the people who live in this home choose to get up at 5 a.m. The principal issue here appears to be lack of choice. By acting in this way the rights of the people who live there are being denied in favour of the staff who work there.

Discrimination is defined as ' ... the process (or set of processes) by which people are allocated to particular social categories with an unequal distribution of rights, resources, opportunities and power' (Thompson, 2003: 82). Discrimination can be experienced by individuals as a result of commission, what we do and say, and omission, what we do not do or say. Discrimination is a powerful force and whether we wish to challenge and even eradicate it '… we cannot remain neutral' (Thompson, 2003: 25). As a social worker, working in a way that is anti-oppressive involves all aspects of practice (for example, at the level of assessment, planning and intervention) and with all service users, whichever service user group you choose to work with. The outcome of discrimination is oppression – 'Inhuman or degrading treatment of individuals … oppression often involves disregarding the rights of an individual or group and is thus a denial of citizenship' (Thompson, 2001: 34).

RESEARCH SUMMARY

*Thompson's (2001) model helps us to understand the interaction between and supports analysis of how inequalities and discrimination feature in the lives of older people. He identifies three levels of analyses: **P**, **C** and **S**.*

P refers to three sub-levels:

1. personal/psychological – individual thoughts, feelings, attitudes and actions;

2. practice – individual interaction with service users;

3. prejudice – inflexibility which stands in the way of judgment.

C refers to the cultural level. This means the shared ways of seeing, thinking and doing, such as what is right and wrong.

S refers to the structure of society, such as social divisions, social forces and socio-political dimensions: connected patterns of power and influence. It is suggested that each of these levels interact with and influence each other.

ACTIVITY **1.9**

Write down a list of examples of how older people may experience discrimination and oppression.

You will have, hopefully, produced a whole variety of examples. Having read an explanation of Thompson's model you could try matching your answers to the different categories. You may have identified personal ways in which older people experience ageism. Examples include a negative approach to individuals such as the use of derogatory or offensive language, seeing a person from the perspective of their chronological age rather than from the perspective of the individual person that they are and suggesting that older people should not have intimate relationships, as well as in older people's negative experience of access to services to support them. You may be aware that some people view social work with older people as 'straightforward' as opposed to the immediacy and complexity of working in childcare. You may know individual older people who have had decisions made for them rather than being consulted about what they want – a 'we know best' mentality. Older people may experience being treated as if they were children. This can be interpreted as seeking to protect that person from harm. However, this may also lead to a denial of those individuals' rights. Cultural ways include language, jokes and images of older people. Structural ways include inequalities in relation to the issues of power and influence that older people have in wider society, for example in relation to employment, housing and access to services such as health and social care. Ageism is both institutionalised in social structures – legally, medically and through welfare, educational and income policies – and internalised in the attitude of individuals.

RESEARCH SUMMARY

The NSF for Older People (Department of Health 2001a) in Standard One: Rooting out age discrimination *provides some examples of evidence of how older people experience age discrimination in certain areas of healthcare and within social care.*

- *Quality of care has been affected by negative staff attitudes in a number of settings.*

- *Many older people and their carers have found that palliative care services have not been available to them.*

- *Councils can discriminate against older people when they apply commissioning strategies that are not sufficiently flexible to take account of individual need.*

- *In some localities eligibility criteria for non-residential services mean older people have had to demonstrate higher needs to qualify for services compared with younger adults.*

- *There is considerable variation across the country in the range of services available to older people and their families or carers.*

- *Older people from black and ethnic minority groups can be particularly disadvantaged and are more likely to suffer discrimination in accessing services.*

Multiple levels of oppression

In considering ageism we need to recognise that some individuals or groups of people may experience multiple oppression through other factors that add to ageist practice. In this section the intention is to focus on issues in relation to class, gender and race and how this impacts upon the lives of older people.

Social class has a major impact on the lives of older people. Social class is linked to income, with those in lower social classes being more likely to live in poverty. Poverty and low income continues to affect a substantial proportion of older people; having an adequate income is a prerequisite for meeting our needs. This means that we are able to afford such things as nutritional food, good housing, heating, mobility, leisure and recreational services. This increases independence, autonomy, choice and participation in the community. The minimum income guaranteed for an older person is, as a proportion of the United Kingdoms average earnings, only 15 per cent. (**www.helptheaged.org.uk**). Additionally, many older people do not take up the benefits that they are entitled to despite sustained efforts to achieve this through advertising and the work of voluntary organisations.

ACTIVITY **1.10**

Consider the following and identify areas of concern and what you consider to be the reasons behind them.

Sarah Ainsworth, 87, has lived in the same house for the last 60 years. It is large and in need of repair. Living off a state pension, she finds it difficult to manage her money, for example covering the cost of heating. Sarah spends most of her time in one room, using the gas fire when she can or wrapping herself in blankets. She has developed a severe cough; the medicines she buys from the local shop do not seem to help. Sarah does not want to visit the doctor; she does not want to be seen as a nuisance. The doctor might suggest things that she cannot afford such as increasing the heating in the house, eating more fruit and vegetables. Sarah would like help with cleaning the house but she has heard that you have to pay for this.

Social disadvantage is associated with increased chances of poor health and reduced life expectancy. People in higher socio-economic classes are more likely to remain healthy and live longer (Graham, 2000). Being poor may mean not being able to heat your home properly, increasing the risk of the individual suffering and poor health. Recovering can be harder without adequate material and social support. For example, an older person may not be able to afford the extra heating or diet required to support recovery. Socially constructed barriers may prevent older people from accessing services. This can be linked to issues of power in relationships, for example feeling that a 'high-status' professional such as a doctor may 'tell you off'. Discriminatory practices can lead people to endure their condition for longer. Stretched and under-resourced services may not focus on preventing change in the person's circumstances, for example through additional home-care support.

In general terms there tend to be more women than men among older people, especially the very old, as women live longer. Women bring to this stage of life their experience of sexism throughout their lives. Sexism may be experienced as low social status and low status in employment with low income. As Mullender (2002) suggests:

> Despite major advances, underpinned by sex discrimination and other legislation, women in Britain still lack equal access to social influence ... women suffer discrimination in relation to education, employment, income, domestic responsibilities, support for caring and social attitudes and expectations throughout all stages of life. (page 298)

This is compounded as they reach older age by the added experience of ageism; Sontag (1978) describes the combination of sexism and ageism as experiencing double discrimination, the 'double standard of ageing'.

In working with any older person it is essential to be socially, politically and culturally 'competent', recognising these different aspects in working with the individual and with communities. This involves developing an understanding of culture, ethnicity, identity and race, particularly as they impact on older people from different ethnic minorities. The experience of racism adds a further dimension to the issues of discrimination and oppression experienced by older people. For example:

> *There is a danger that assessment will be based on dominant white norms without adequate attention being paid to cultural differences ... social work assessment needs to be based on understanding and analysis rather than ignorance and assumptions. (Thompson, 2001: 73)*

As a social worker you need to take into account the experience of a person who is black by recognising diversity and difference and his or her experience as an older person. In particular this group may experience 'triple jeopardy' (Norman, 1985) – ageism, racism and a low socio-economic position in relation to class.

The issue of social exclusion has increased prominence, particularly through the current political agenda. Both at a national and a European level the social inclusion agenda acknowledges that 'poverty' is not just about having insufficient money but about multi-faceted levels of disadvantage and oppression. People and groups become 'excluded', for example because of their income, because they are unemployed or have a low-income job, because of race, culture, class, ill-health, disability and so on. This may have an effect on access to services such as health provision and educational opportunities. The concept of 'citizenship' seeks to place the rights and duties of individuals as part of wider society. This may be demonstrated through consultation, participation and control by the individual or groups to make and implement decisions. This issue is discussed further in Chapter 3.

Anti-discriminatory practice

How can we begin to challenge our views and assumptions and those of others about older people? Hopefully you will have already begun to reflect on this through reading this chapter and will continue to do so as you progress through this book. Challenging and evaluating your views and assumptions, both professionally and personally, through reflective practice must be a critical feature of your professional life. Being open and critical of our own practice is an essential way to learn. In promoting anti-discriminatory practice in relation to older people, it is essential that this is not seen in isolation from the experience of other service user groups. There is an interrelationship between different aspects of discrimination and oppression, for example as we have already seen in relation to sexism and racism. Anti-oppressive practice must be part of wider reflection on good practice in social work.

Empowerment is an essential feature of good practice in all social work and is a critical feature of overcoming oppression. This is about helping people to gain control over their lives. Banks (2001) points out that this has a range of meanings:

> *... from giving users some limited choice (the consumerist approach) to power sharing (the citizenship approach) to supporting and encouraging people or groups to realise their own power and take action for themselves (a 'radical' approach'). (pages 131–2)*

ACTIVITY **1.11**

Consider the following:

Sarah Ainsworth, whom you met in Activity 1.10, was admitted into hospital with pneu-monia. Her health is improving and plans need to be made in relation to her future care. Sarah's daughter wants her to go into a home for older people, close to where she lives. 'This means that I can visit mum everyday. I'll know she will be safe.' Other people involved with Sarah also feel that this would be the best course of action. Sarah wants to go home. However she feels that she 'does not stand a chance against everyone else.'

How might you empower Sarah?

In working with any person, it is essential to understand the individual's perspective on their position. For older people, this may include how they experience 'ageism' and its impact on them. Older people may be supported to 'adjust' to the circumstances that they are in. This could be viewed as part of a reductionism approach – '... the process of reduc-ing a complex, multi-faceted reality to a simple, single-level explanation' (Thompson, 2003: 150). We need to acknowledge that ageism and ageist practice can have the effect of demoralising an individual, making them feel useless and marginalised. You need to consider how ageism may influence your practice. For example, in undertaking assess-ments of people there is a tendency to focus on 'need' rather than the strengths and the contribution that an individual can make.

Ageist practice may also include the use of certain terminology.

ACTIVITY **1.12**

You visit Sarah on the ward. One of your colleagues is talking to her. She says: 'Here she is, darling. Your special friend. She is a sweet old thing, aren't you, Sarah? No trouble at all. You're our "little darling".'

How do you feel about the way that this person is talking about Sarah? Why might your colleague feel this is appropriate? What do you think that you should do?

In using the language that she does, this person is reducing the relationship to one that could be seen to be patronising. It can be difficult to challenge – the person may consider themselves as being positive and well-meaning. You could choose to challenge this now but this may be difficult as Sarah may be embarrassed or indeed appear not to mind being talked to in this way. You may wish to explore with Sarah when you are on your own with her asking how she feels about the way that the person spoke to her and, if appropriate, consider ways in which she could challenge this approach in a way that she feels comfort-able with. You could talk to the person yourself, acknowledging the intention but asking the person to consider what impact this may have on the individual. It is always hard to challenge the views of another person. However, this does not have to be confrontational; it could be explorative with you seeking to outline your views and opinion while listening

ask family about patronising

to the views of the other person. The approach taken by the member of staff is the opposite end of the continuum from ageism – anti-ageist positivism (Bytheway, 1995: 128). Thoughts such as 'older people are so sweet', 'some of them are such characters' and so on could be considered another way of labelling and oppressing individuals. This may be internalised by the older person, particularly if they are feeling ill, unhappy or sad, and consequently could lead to dependency and compliance by the individual.

Ageist practice can be seen in the way that people are labelled as one homegenous group such as 'the elderly'. This could be viewed as depersonalising – it is essential to focus on the individual. Talking about people who are older or older people avoids a protective approach. It also seeks to understand the individual's perspective on the reality of their life and the unique contribution of their life and life course.

Empowerment '... involves helping people to gain greater control of their lives and circumstances' (Thompson, 2002: 91). A critical feature of empowerment is understanding the nature of power, especially as the service user perceives this. This may be ascribed to a particular status or certain professionals, for example consultants within a hospital. Power and the perception of power by the older person will be demonstrated in the authority that professionals hold with regard to their interventions and duties in relation to legislation, policy and guidance, decision-making, access to resources and so on. Consequently the key tasks of the professional must be to promote the individual's dignity through enhancing their self-esteem and self-worth. This should be based on meaningful dialogue with the person, listening to and talking with the person, recognising their strengths and reinforcing their rights. The legitimate use of power lies in challenging discrimination and oppression.

C H A P T E R   S U M M A R Y

In this chapter you have had the opportunity to consider your views on ageism – the values and attitudes that you hold. We have considered issues of discrimination and oppression and how older people might experience these, particularly as older people may experience multiple oppression. You will also have considered how you might promote practice that is anti-oppressive.

The reality of age is right before our eyes. There are unmistakable differences between the appearance of a person who is 80 years old and that of a person who is 20 years old. Being older can mean that you may be more experienced, frail, less physically and mentally able to achieve things. Working in a way that is ageist makes assumptions that there are universal changes that come with age that have a negative impact upon people's lives. As an attempt to distance ourselves both personally and institutionally from those seen as different, we allow those negative connotations to pervade our understanding of later adulthood. Clearly we need to challenge this.

Theories and models of working with older people are valid and important; they provide an essential framework for understanding and conceptualising your work. The integration of theory and practice is critical to the development of professional social work practice. What we are seeking to do is to remind you of the importance of acknowledging individual difference and diversity and understanding the significance that these differences may have for working with older people.

Banks, S. (2001) *Ethics and Values in Social Work*, 2nd edn. Basingstoke: Palgrave Macmillan.
This book provides a comprehensive analysis of the issues and dilemmas for social workers in understanding and implementing their values within their practice.

Bytheway, B. (1995) *Ageism*. Buckingham: Open University Press.
This book examines the issues of ageism by exploring the way in which age is viewed within our culture, rejecting the concept of old age. It provides examples of ageism in everyday practice.

Thompson, N. (2001) *Anti-Discriminatory Practice*, 3rd edn. Basingstoke: Palgrave Macmillan.
This book explores the main areas of discrimination and how those working in social care can challenge the complex forms of discrimination, inequality and oppression. One chapter examines the issue of ageism.

www.dictionary.com

www.topps.org.uk

www.gscc.org.uk

Chapter 2
The changing context of social work practice with older people

This chapter will help you to begin to meet the following National Occupational Standards:

Key Role 1: Prepare for and work with individuals, families, carers, groups and communities to assess their needs and circumstances
- Prepare for social work contact and involvement
- Work with individuals, families, carers, groups and communities to help them make informed decisions

Key Role 3: Support individuals to represent their needs, views and circumstances
- Advocate with, and on behalf of, individuals, families, carers, groups and communities

Key Role 5: Manage and be accountable with supervision and support for your own social work practice within your organisation
- Manage and be accountable for your own work
- Work within multi-disciplinary and multi-organisational teams, networks and systems

Key Role 6: Demonstrate professional competence in social work practice
- Work within agreed standards of social work practice and ensure own professional development
- Manage complex ethical issues, dilemmas and conflicts

It will also introduce you to the following academic standards as set out in the social work subject benchmark statement:

3.1.1 Social work services and service users
- The social processes (associated with, for example, poverty, unemployment, poor health, disablement, lack of education and other sources of disadvantage) that lead to marginalisation, isolation and exclusion and their impact on the demands for social work services

3.1.2 The service delivery context
- The location of contemporary social work within both historical and comparative perspectives, including European and international contexts

3.1.3 Values and ethics
- The moral concepts of rights, responsibility, freedom, authority and power inherent in the practice of social workers as moral and statutory agents
- Aspects of philosophical ethics relevant to the understanding and resolution of value dilemmas and conflicts in both interpersonal and professional contexts

The subject skills highlighted to demonstrate this knowledge in practice include:
- Listen actively to others, engage appropriately with the life experiences of service users, understand accurately their viewpoint and overcome personal prejudices to respond appropriately to a range of complex personal and interpersonal situations
- Consult actively with others, including service users, who hold relevant information or expertise
- Analyse and take account of the impact of inequality and discrimination in work with people in particular contexts and problem situations
- Ability to use this knowledge and understanding in work within specific practice contexts

Introduction

By developing the discussion about the position of older people in society from Chapter 1, this chapter will consider how the cultural, economic and social context of being an older person impacts upon and influences social work practice and services with older people. It will locate contemporary social work practice with older people within both historical and comparative perspectives, including European and international perspectives. Thus in this chapter you will consider the context of social work practice with older people. You will be encouraged to examine how service delivery and practice may be influenced by the way in which ageing is conceptualised in our society.

Being an older person

As we have already seen from Chapter 1, older people are often seen as separate – as a distinct group who should be set apart simply because of age. We see this, for example, in the language used towards older people and in the images that are presented of them. Negative images of older people lead to discrimination and oppression, supporting the social exclusion and marginalisation of individuals and groups of older people. This is further reinforced through issues in relation to the influence of such issues as class, gender, ethnicity and poverty. Ageing as a process can be addressed from a biological or psychological perspective but, as we have already suggested, the definition of old age is largely a social construction. As Hockey and James (2003) suggest, '… experiences of … growing old emerge out of culturally specific assumptions about the shape and nature of the life course' (page 130). The social construction of older people is powerful in its influences on the way that age is perceived and responded to within our society. Consequently examining the social response to the needs of older people will support you in determining the way that older people are perceived and how these perceptions influence our practice and response.

> *Welfare responses are expressions of the social values attached to old age as much as of the material infrastructure within which old age is experienced. Any structured social response to ageing necessarily combines images of older people with ideas about the rights, needs and contributions of older members of society. (Hugman, 1994: 152)*

It is a fact that the proportion of people aged 60 or over has increased throughout the world. The population of the United Kingdom is getting older. Demographic changes in the population mean that the numbers of older people have increased dramatically. People are living longer due to such issues as improved healthcare and improved living conditions in the social environment. In addition the birth rate has fallen with fewer babies being born with a consequent fall in the number of young people entering the labour market.

RESEARCH SUMMARY

- *In 1900 4 per cent of the population in England was aged 60 or over.*
- *In 1971, just over 13 per cent of the population in England was aged 60 or over.*
- *In 2003, 21 per cent of the population in England was aged 60 or over.*
- *By 2011, 16.6 per cent of the population in England is expected to be aged 65 or over.*
- *By 2020, 25 per cent of the population in the United Kingdom is expected to be aged 65 years and over.*
- *By 2031 29 per cent of the population in England is expected to be aged over 60.*

Source: ***www.gad.gov.uk***

The most significant increase will be in the number of people aged 85 years and over, who will be three times more than in the 1990s. These trends offer many challenges. Professionals involved in health and welfare services for older people have to consider the planning of services to meet the needs of a growing number of older people. Attention needs to be focused on the experience of older people, in particularly the experience among many of a poor quality of life. The perspective on these trends has been to depict the growing number of older people in the population as 'a disaster', 'a crisis' and an increasing burden upon society. The 'elderly' are perceived as a problem, placing the individual older person potentially in a dependent role.

ACTIVITY 2.1

- *Consider what you wish from your later adulthood.*
- *What do you hope to be doing? How would you expect to be treated?*

It is probable that you have a hope that your later adulthood would be as positive and fulfilling as possible. As we grow older we want to stay healthy and independent; we want to be treated equally and fairly; we want services that meet our needs which are not tied up in bureaucratic systems and processes. The suggestion is that as we grow older our fundamental needs stay the same. People do not want to be viewed as at the end of their life but rather be perceived as individuals who have had a whole range of experiences and have a continuing valid contribution to make to society. A focus on planning and providing services that meet the needs of individual people who are older focuses on participation, involvement and ensuring that the individual is fully informed.

> ### RESEARCH SUMMARY
>
> *Social production function theory (SPF) asserts that people produce their own well-being by trying to optimise, within the constraints they are facing, the achievement of two universal goals – physical well-being and social approval. There is a need to maintain both physical and social well-being in order to age successfully.*
>
> *Physical well-being has two dimensions:*
>
> - *Comfort refers to the absence of thirst, hunger, pain and so on.*
>
> - *Stimulation refers to activities that produce arousal – social and physical activities.*
>
> *Social well-being has three dimensions:*
>
> - *Status refers to relative 'ranking' that is based on education, social origin and capabilities. Qualities associated with this dimension include being treated respectfully, self-realisation, having a good reputation.*
>
> - *Behavioural confirmation refers to social skills and social networks and is defined as positive feedback on behaviour by others and self-approval. Qualities associated with this dimension include doing the right thing and a sense of belonging to a functional group.*
>
> - *Affection includes love, friendship and emotional support. Qualities associated with this dimension include liking and being liked, trust and being trusted, reciprocal empathy, a sense of loving and being loved.*
>
> *Steverink et al. (1998) propose as a minimum requirement for successful ageing that at least one of the instrumental goals in each of the domains of physical and social well-being must be met. They suggest they are usually comfort and affection.*

Elaborations of these concepts stress the importance of a biographical approach to successful ageing. They suggest that the quality of life cannot be simply understood in the light of current circumstances but recognise the influence of the life that has been lived by the older person in giving meaning to their later adulthood (Ruth and Oberg 1996). Nilsson et al. (1998) in a study of over-60 older people argue that what creates a perception of a 'good life' in older age is related to:

- personal relationships – a feeling of belonging, usually, but not exclusively, within a family context;

- activity – engaging in meaningful activity and a feeling of being needed;

- links between past and present lives, where the past and future, however short, are viewed positively;

- a philosophy of life based on religious or other strong, personal beliefs.

What are the implications of these studies for practice with older people? They do provide us with a framework to explore the quality of an individual's past and current life and their aspirations for the future. This means paying attention to the individual experiences, values and perceptions of older people in supporting a meaningful life in older age. This includes recognising our own attitudes and values towards older people and valuing and enjoying the work undertaken with older people (Nolan, 1997). However, it is important to note that these elements focus on the individual factors of ageing. We should also consider the impact of structural factors on older people.

Historical context of social work practice with older people

The way in which we have responded to the needs of older people through history appears to be a powerful determinant of the present culture of care for older people in England.

In the Middle Ages care was largely dependent on religious institutions with some charitable institutional care within larger towns. With the Reformation and the consequent dissolution of the monastic system, this left little or no care for those who required it. The roots of the current systems of care could be said to lie in the Poor Law Act of 1601. This law placed the responsibility of care on the local community, with individual care being institutionalised within the parish boundaries. This decision to place the responsibility of care for older people with the community rather than the family was a consequence of living in an agriculture-based society. The failure of a harvest was often beyond the control of the individual. However, a failed crop also meant that people could not earn any money. Therefore it was perceived that the parish had to take care of older people. 'Being on the parish' was a demeaning status for many older people (Foote and Stanners, 2002).

The development of workhouses, originally founded by the Quakers, was intended to promote self-help through communes of care. With no formal welfare system, older people who were deemed to be paupers often found themselves housed within the workhouse. Over the years, as more people were housed there who were sick, disabled or seen as in need of correctional reform, workhouses increasingly were seen as a place for needy, unproductive members of the community. Regimes within these workhouses were frequently harsh. The Industrial Revolution with the growth of large towns saw even greater pressure on these systems of care and their increasing costs. In an attempt to control the costs, the Poor Law Amendment Act of 1834 abolished outdoor relief and anybody requiring help had to be admitted to the workhouse. For older people, especially those who were poor, this left them with little choice or control over their lives. Within these systems and the values that underpinned them, older people were seen as a burden on society. The Royal Commission on the Aged Poor (1895), chaired by Lord Aberdare, provided evidence of the poor condition in which many older people existed. While it suggested that workhouse conditions should be improved for older people, it considered outdoor relief as adequate and did not recommend any major changes.

By the beginning of the twentieth century there was little provision for the needs of older people, with any care being through the Poor Law, almshouses and workhouses. However, change was in the air. In 1901 Seebohm Rowntree published a report in which he distinguished between primary and secondary poverty. He considered primary poverty to be caused by low pay and secondary poverty as, even when earnings were sufficient, spending was wasteful. He criticised the current systems and called for action to fight the problems of unemployment and support for those who were ill and for those in old age. Influenced by these findings the government passed the Old Age Pension Act in 1908, which provided a pension of up to five shillings a week for people over 70 years of age with incomes of less than £31 10 shillings a year. However, the general view was that most people wanted to stay in some kind of employment until they were physically unable to do so. Consequently the experience of older age was to work or to be seen as too frail or stupid to work and therefore perceived as 'useless'.

The Royal Commission on the Poor of 1909, following four years of extensive investigation, further emphasised the poor conditions and treatment of older people. The Commission was famously split and its recommendations were published as two reports. The Majority Report recommended the creation of a new Poor Law, replacing the workhouse with specialised institutions for groups such as children, those who were mentally ill and older people. The Minority report, signed by four members, Beatrice Webb, George Lansbury, Revd Wakefield and Mr F. Chandler, advocated the complete break up of the Poor Laws and its functions transferred to other authorities; the emphasis was on prevention of destitution rather than its relief. With no major inquiries and publication between the First and Second World Wars it would appear that the welfare of older people was deemed as having a low priority within society. The Local Government Act 1929 transferred the powers and duties of Poor Law Guardians to county councils and boroughs, who took over the running of some of the institutions with others managed by public assistance committees of local councils. However, conditions remained poor.

During the Second World War feelings grew within society that there should not automatically be a divide between the rich ('givers') and the poor ('takers'); social problems were beginning to be seen no longer as the fault of the individual but to lie in the social context. The landmark report *Social Insurance and Allied Services* (Beveridge, 1942) laid the foundations for a welfare state that was more socially just, materially equal and more democratic. Under the National Health Service Act 1946 a comprehensive health service was set up to deliver improvements in health and to provide effective services, with access to those services regardless of means, for example groups such as those receiving a pension were exempt from paying prescription charges. This Act enabled local authorities to promote the welfare of people who were 'deaf, dumb, blind or substantially handicapped' through the provision of workshops, hostels and recreational provision, with older people who came under these categories also being able to benefit from them. Funds could be given by local authorities to voluntary organisations providing meals or recreation facilities for older people. Under Part III of this Act local authorities could make available accommodation to those who by reason of their age, infirmity or other circumstances could not care for themselves. Welfare services developed in a gradual way with welfare officers largely delivering the range of services developed from the Poor Law, although in 1948 new children's departments emerged, staffed by professional childcare officers.

In the 1960s there was growing concern about the cost of services, in particular as a result of duplication and the fragmentation of services which failed to meet the needs of the people. The Seebohm Report of 1968 recommended a generic service and the 1970s saw social services move towards a more integrated approach. Additionally the NHS was restructured in 1974 with healthcare concentrated in the Health Service and expertise in social care in social services departments.

Since the 1970s and especially since the Conservatives, under the leadership of Margaret Thatcher, came into power in 1979, there has been a questioning of the role of the state in providing care. The state has never been the sole provider of welfare provision as voluntary and independent providers have always played a role. A major reason for questioning the growing role of the state in providing welfare services is the increasing cost. The emphasis during the 'Thatcher years' was on providing care in a market economy or 'welfare pluralism', with a move away from state provision towards the contracting out of services to the independent sector. Prominence was on giving more choice for the individual and that personal responsibility should be encouraged.

Moving towards community care

One of the main developments in the last 50 years, with an accelerated growth in the last 20 years, has been a move away from care provided in institutions to care in the community for older people.

ACTIVITY **2.2**

Make a list of the reasons for the move towards care in the community of older people?

The reasons for the move towards care in the community of older people are multi-faceted. They could be summarised as being economic, political and social. From the 1950s onwards there was a growing concern about the experience of older people receiving institutional care, with concerns about the poor quality of care given to older people and the poor quality of care staff providing this care. Research by Townsend (1962) detailed the poor quality of experience of older people, concluding that long-stay institutions should be abandoned in favour of a move towards living in the community. The response was to increase capital investment in the building of modern residential homes, with the political belief that this type of care was cheaper than care of older people in the National Health Services (Means et al., 2002). With a change to social security regulations in the early 1980s which made it easier for people to claim supplementary benefits (now income support) towards the cost of their residential care, the cost of caring for older people in residential care was of growing concern. Victor (1997) states that the number of residential and nursing home places provided by the independent sector increased from 46,900 in 1982 to 161,200 by 1991. Expenditure on placements in these homes increased from £10 million (1979) to £1,872 million (1991) (page 14). Additionally there is seen to be less need to keep some individuals in institutions as improvements in health and medication have supported the control of behaviour that was previously seen as bizarre and/or difficult. From a social perspective it is suggested that there is a positive benefit in relation to quality of life in living at home. Faced with criticism about increased cost, the concerns for quality of care offered in residential homes and the political rhetoric of questioning the role of the state in providing care, the policy and legal context of health and social care policy has continued, and continues, to constantly change, emphasising initiatives towards care within the community. These issues and subsequent legal and political developments are examined further in Chapter 3.

The experience of older people

In the first part of this chapter you looked at the demographic evidence that the population of the United Kingdom is getting older. You examined a psychological dimension of
growing older and factors which may support a healthy approach to and experience of
older age. You were reminded that there are structural issues that contribute to the experience of later adulthood. By taking a historical perspective of the development of services
for older people and their experience of them, you will have considered the foundation for
the development of current services, in particular the reasons that underpin the development of community care services for older people.

In this part of the chapter you will learn about the experience of older people through
examining the structural factors in society that influence their experience of later adulthood. This builds on Chapter 1 in which you examined the way in which social differences
affected the social positions of older people in society, that is social class, gender and
ethnic difference.

ACTIVITY 2.3

*Mabel was 80 years of age in 1904. Joan was 80 years of age in 2004. List the possible
differences and similarities of their social experience of being an older person.*

One hundred years span the differences in experience of these women. You may have
identified a range of differences in social experience. Both women will have lived through
great changes in society, Mabel in relation to the industrial revolution and Joan in relation
to the technological revolution. Joan will have experienced the changing position and role
of women. If both women were part of the wealthy classes they will have experienced the
advantages of money and subsequent ability to have a relatively secure older age.
However, if these women were from working-class backgrounds they are more likely to
have experienced financial, health and daily living challenges associated with poor income.
Both will be subject to the stereotypes and oppressive and discriminatory attitudes that
society attributes to older people. Despite relative social and economic changes in the
intervening one hundred years older people are still experiencing hardship.

RESEARCH SUMMARY

*The Independent Inquiry into Inequalities in Health (1999), chaired by Sir Donald Acheson
found:*

- *older people were more likely to be living in poverty;*

- *the poorest pensioners have experienced a relative decline in their income;*

- *older people are at risk of fuel poverty;*

- *older people experience a disproportionate lack of access to transport.*

As we have already noted, older people do not make up a homogeneous group. Some, particularly among the group of younger older people have a reasonable life style, living in good housing and enjoying good health. Others can be socially isolated, living on low incomes in poor housing and experiencing poor health.

Older people who are 75 years and more, particularly women living alone, have the lowest incomes. They rely more on benefits as a source of their income and receive a smaller proportion of their income from occupational pensions and investments. At all ages, women have a lower income than men. In 1998, 48 per cent of single women aged 60–64 and 68 per cent of single women aged 85 and over were living on just their state pension and income support. Many older people who are eligible for income support do not claim it (**www.ageconcern.org.uk**). Over the last 20 years, compared with a rise of 50 per cent in average earnings, older people dependent on benefits have experienced a relative deterioration in their income that has risen only marginally compared with average earnings. In general, the majority of the older population live on very limited means (**www.dti.gov.uk**).

For most people over retirement age, leisure activity generally decreases. Several barriers have been identified which prevent older people from participating in the more active leisure pursuits. These include health and mobility problems, poor transport facilities and lack of finance.

Living alone has become more common among older people. Generations of families no longer tend to live together; children are more likely to move away from their parents. The probability of needing domiciliary care or care in a nursing/residential home is greater among people who live alone.

RESEARCH SUMMARY

- *16% of all households consisted of a lone person aged 60 or over, with women aged 60 years and over forming the largest proportion.*

- *34% of women and 19% of men in the 65–74 age group lived alone.*

- *59% of women and 29% of men in the 75 and over age group lived alone.*

Source: ***www.age2000.org.uk***

With the decline in marriage and rise in separation and divorce, it is likely that the numbers of single households will continue to increase.

The majority of long-term care of older people is still provided informally by families with 1 in 8 adults providing such care. In Great Britain there are estimated to be 3.3 million (61 per cent) women carers and 2.4 million male carers with over half of all carers caring for people aged 75 years or over (**www.ageconcern.org.uk**). The increasing numbers of working women means less time is available for caring for their older relatives. Changes in marriage and fertility patterns (the trend towards having children later), the increase in longevity as well as the rise in divorce, cohabitation and single parenthood are also likely to impact on both household structure and availability of the care which family members provide. With competing family obligations people may not have the same capacity, in terms of finances or living space, to accommodate or care for an older member of the family (Office for National Statistics, 1999).

It is clear that older people from black and minority ethnic communities are not achieving equal access to social, health, and economic services. Their numbers are also increasing significantly: by 2030, the minority elder population in the UK will have increased tenfold, from 175,000 to over 1.7 million. The greatest part of that increase will take place in the next 15 years (Schuman, 1999).

Older people are often excluded from universal access to services. Social exclusion refers to 'a shorthand term for what can happen when people or areas suffer from a combination of linked problems such as unemployment, poor skills, low incomes, poor housing, high crime environments, bad health and family breakdown' (**www.socialexclusionunit.gov.uk**). Many older people are at disproportionate risk of falling into poverty and are subject to discrimination in employment. Many rely on public transport and research has shown that a lack of mobility can prevent older people from participating in social activities and lead to low morale, depression and loneliness (**www.helptheaged.org.uk**). Many older people find themselves in unsuitable housing for their needs.

RESEARCH SUMMARY

The policy document Housing for Older People *(Housing Corporation, 2002) identifies the experience of social exclusion by older people through a lack of social contact or through living in inaccessible and isolating environments. The challenge is to develop a range of housing and services that meets the need of the whole community and that promotes age equality and social inclusion. The Corporation's strategy document* Strategy for Housing Older People in England *(2003) sets out its vision for investment in a range of affordable housing and services which will improve older people's quality of life by giving them greater choice and control over where and how they live, promoting greater independence, interdependence and social inclusion.*

The development of the 'Supporting People' initiative is intended to help vulnerable people live in mainstream housing by enabling them to access support services. (Based on **www.spkweb.org.uk***)*

Healthcare inequalities still remain in the treatment and care of older people. One response from the government has been the development of the National Service Framework for Older People (DoH, 2001a), which sets a programme of reform and targets to create health and welfare services to meet the needs of older people. This is examined in Chapter 3 and in other chapters.

The challenges for work with older people

In the following chapter in particular and in the subsequent chapters of this book you will be able to develop your understanding of the political, legal and social response to the challenges of responding to and caring for a growing population of older people. Throughout this book you will be examining the different theories, models and concepts of practice with older people. How should you conceptualise and understand your role as a social worker? National Occupational Standards and Subject Benchmarks for Social work, identified at the beginning of every chapter, are one way of beginning to understand your role as a social worker with older people. In this section the ways in which your practice may be influenced by the way in which ageing is conceptualised by society are examined.

ACTIVITY 2.4

Pauline is 70 years of age. In the last two years her health and mobility have deteriorated significantly and she finds it difficult to care for herself. The house in which she lives is old and in need of repair, but Pauline has no money to fix things. Pauline feels old and useless. She wants to live in her own home but believes that she has no choice but to move into a home for older people. Pauline has a learning disability and has lived independently for the last 30 years, following her marriage to Leonard.

She remembers the way in which people tried to stop them getting married; one of her aunties refused to come to the wedding saying it was not right that 'their sort' married. Until his death last year she and Leonard had shared a happy marriage though they had their ups and downs and it was difficult living on benefits. For a couple of years Pauline had a job as a waitress in a café. She had really enjoyed the job but had had to give it up when standing up became difficult because of a deteriorating condition in her knees. Now no one seems to care. Her niece visits occasionally but she is busy with two small children and a full-time job.

Pauline finds going out a big problem. The shops are some distance away and transport links are poor; even when she gets to the shops she finds it difficult to walk around. Two weeks ago, she tripped and fell, and was lucky she only had a few cuts and bruises. She finds everything very expensive and some days has no food in the house at all. Lately the neighbourhood in which she lives has been getting very noisy; every night her street has gangs of young people hanging around. Pauline is frightened of them and worried that they might break in so she often sits in the dark with no television on so they will think nobody is home. When her General Practitioner visited her last week following her fall, she said that she would get a social worker to visit. Pauline is unsure how this person can help her.

List the ways in which cultural, economic and social aspects impact on Pauline's life.

We would suggest that Pauline's experience of quality of life is poor. Culturally she finds herself marginalised; she appears to be isolated and lonely, having little contact with others. She is frightened of going out and is fearful at home. Her health problems compound her feelings of isolation and of 'uselessness'. Economically she finds herself living on a low income that appears to be insufficient to meet her needs and in housing in need of repair. Socially her only contact appears to be with her niece, who is only able to visit occasionally. These factors compound her social isolation and vulnerability.

Social workers have a major contribution to make in understanding the impact of individual, social and structural issues on the life of an older person and on the lives of older people in general and how this is experienced through 'ageism', that is discrimination because of age. Pauline has experienced oppression and discrimination throughout her life and in later adulthood, which leaves her feeling old and useless, that she no longer has a place in society or a contribution to make. Through listening to Pauline's past and current experiences you will gain a greater understanding of what she has been through and her emotions. You will need to find out what is important to Pauline. In working with Pauline you will provide a range of social support. You need to acknowledge her vulnerability. At a personal level this will involve seeking to understand and acknowledge her experiences of loss – the death of her husband, her feelings of unhappiness and despair. This will also involve a wider understanding of Pauline's experiences within society – her feelings about the community and the threats and opportunities that she feels it offers her. In undertaking this you need to identify her strengths – the things that she has achieved and continues to achieve in her life. You are helping her to make sense of her own life and make her own choices. Through empowering her to make choices for herself you are supporting Pauline in not being a passive recipient but an active participant in assessment and planning to meet her own needs.

Comparative perspectives

The population of the world is getting older with the vast majority of older people living in the developing world.

RESEARCH SUMMARY

The World Health Organisation states that:

- *In 2000, there were 600 million people aged 60 and over; there will be 1.2 billion by 2025 and 2 billion by 2050 (see Figure 2.1).*

- *Today, about 66 per cent of all older people are living in the developing world; by 2025, it will be 75 per cent.*

- *In the developed world, the very old (age 80+) is the fastest growing population group.*

- *Women outlive men in virtually all societies; consequently in very old age, the ratio of women to men is 2:1.*

Source: **www.who.int/ageing**

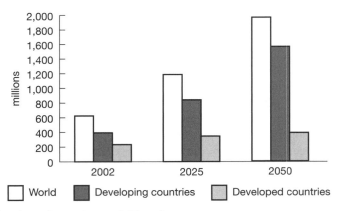

Figure 2.1 *Number of people aged 60 and over*

Europe has an identity separate from that of other continents, such as Africa and Asia. There is to a certain degree a sense of shared history and of cultural origin, for example in Judaeo-Christian traditions. The emergence of a European identity has increasingly become integrated in economic, political, social and cultural exchange, especially under the auspices of the European Union (EU).

RESEARCH SUMMARY

- *There are more than 70 million people aged 60 and over living in the EU, representing just under one in five of the population.*

- *Nearly one-third of the EU's population and one-fifth of the labour force are over the age of 50.*

- *By 2020 about 20 million people will be aged 80 and over – representing an increase of 300 per cent in this age category since 1960.*

Source: **www.europa.eu.int**

How can the study of the care of older people in other countries inform our practice? Considering social welfare provision in other countries gives you an opportunity to learn about other forms of welfare provision. It also gives you an opportunity to question and analyse your own practice – why do we practice as we do? What values underpin this practice and how and why might they be different from those in another country? What historical, political and social aspects have influenced the development of practice in England as compared to another country (Hetherington, 2001)? Studying the experiences of older people in other countries allows you to identify and examine similarity, diversity and difference among themes. An example would be the different social and political concepts of family relationships in and obligation for the care of older people; this could include the issues of abuse and neglect balanced with the regard in which older people are held within families, communities and the wider society. As Anttonen et al. (2003) suggest, social care models vary because of the history of welfare institutions and 'the norms and assumptions that govern social care in a locality are also the products of cultural, political and particular religious values' (page 15).

One way of classifying social work and its roles and tasks is to examine the link to the welfare regime and the state's approach and response to its citizens (Lorenz, 1994). One way of examining this is to look at the state's approach from a historical perspective, as we have done in this chapter. As we are demonstrating throughout this book social work and the development of services are inextricably linked to political, economic, social and cultural factors. Examining welfare regimes in other countries gives you an opportunity to 'locate' and further understand the model of delivery in England in a wider context.

RESEARCH SUMMARY

Esping-Andersen (1996) outlines the following models of welfare systems:

- Liberal or neo-liberal. *These welfare systems rely on market-based social insurance approaches to financial provision, with relatively low state benefits for the poor and needy as these are primarily seen to be disincentives for work. Private forms of welfare are encouraged to allow people to have more than the bare minimum. Examples that are given include the United States of America and the United Kingdom.*

- Conservative corporatist. *The state is important but not usually in a direct fashion. Financial provision for welfare services relies more on social insurance rather than purely on taxation. The family, particularly 'traditional' family forms, is important and the state only intervenes when the family cannot resolve its own problems. Examples that are given include Austria, France and Germany.*

- Social democratic or Scandinavian. *The dominant principles in these systems are universalism, social solidarity and equality across all classes. The state fulfils many family responsibilities so that people have more opportunity to work. Benefits are provided by the state through high taxation and therefore the model depends on opportunities for full employment. Examples that are given include the Scandinavian countries.*

These models offer a starting point. However, welfare systems are a dynamic process with changing forms.

In this next section you will consider examples of welfare provision from each of the models described by Esping-Andersen – the United States of America (USA), Germany and Denmark.

Within the *United States* there is a largely market-driven system of social care supported by voluntary and denominational provision. Health and social care needs are initially the responsibility of individuals and their families, with needs being met in the health and social care market. However, in the case of older people in the United States there is generous use of Medicaid, the key source of health and social care payments. These are federal/state entitlement programmes that pay for medical assistance for individuals and families with low income and resources.

Barbara, aged 88, has lived in a private nursing home in Long Beach, California for two years. Following her husband's death when she was 77 she moved to a retirement community in Long Beach to be nearer her daughter. Initially, she was able to care for herself in her own home. When Barbara's health began to deteriorate her daughter helped her out and Barbara was able to employ a private home carer to assist her. However, when her health deteriorated further she moved into the home, which she chose with the help of her family. Initially she was able to pay for the fees herself but her money soon ran out and her costs are now met by Medicare.

As in Britain, current patterns of providing social care services in *Germany* have grown out of the poor laws. It is traditionally assumed that the family will support older relatives. Most care for older people in Germany is provided by informal carers, usually families and especially women. A major part of social services is provided by charities, which co-operate with local authorities. There are six major associations operating within an umbrella organisation – *Bundesarbeitsgemeinschaft der Freien Wohlfahrtspflege*. Traditionally there are a considerable number of people working on a voluntary basis with welfare agencies which raise income through donations, memberships, foundations and so on, and from church taxes in the case of those organisations associated with the church. However, the majority of their income is through state grants and service charges. The most important legal base for people in need of care is the *Soziale Pflegeversicherung* or 'Long-Term Care Insurance Law' (LTCI), passed in April 1995. It is funded by the contributions of employers and employees, with entitlements also given to spouses and children. It covers 99 per cent of the population, with the main users being older people. This care insurance system entitles those covered to make a choice between benefits in cash or in kind; for example, they may choose to pay relatives rather than professional providers. The LTCI reinforces family care by providing protection to informal carers, including a yearly holiday and the payment of pension contributions. There is also provision for advice centres and support groups. The LCTI provides definitions of need on which the bases of care are assessed. These assessments of need are made by doctors according to strict criteria. Community and institutional services are largely provided by various non-governmental and not-for-profit organisations on the basis of general contracts. About 5 per cent of the population who are over 65 years of age live in institutional care, just over half in nursing homes and the rest in residential care homes (**www.bmfsj.de**).

Ully, aged 92, lives in a flat in her daughter's house. Her daughter provides for her care needs and Ully uses her care insurance to pay towards this. This means that her daughter only has to work part-time and they are able to spend time together. Once a week Ully attends a local social centre for older people which is run and funded by her church. When her daughter takes her holiday, paid for from the insurance, home care and meals on wheels are provided by one of the local voluntary organisations. Ully also has daily visits from one of the church volunteers.

Since the early 1980s *Denmark* has adhered to the principle of maintaining people in their own home rather than in residential care, with older people receiving the necessary help to live independently of their families. This has led to the expansion of home care. The provision of home helps (*Hjemmehjaelp*) is intended to ensure that older people are supported in their own home. Day centres (*Dagcenter*) focus on social aspects of life. Housing benefits for the majority of older people are generous. Special public housing such as service flats, sheltered housing and housing collectivism form part of the Danish policy. The health of older Danes is generally good as they lead active lifestyles. According to Giarchi (1996) there is no stigma attached to approaching social services as '... the Danes are socialised into the ethos of state welfare provision and their social services are amongst the best in the world' (page 99). There is heavy investment in social care through taxation and expectations as to rights to receive services are high.

CASE STUDY

Anders, aged 85, has lived in supported housing following the death of his wife two years ago. He has a home help twice a week, who cleans for him and, if she has time, does some cooking. A warden lives on the site and usually visits him once a day to make sure he is alright; if Anders needs him he can contact him directly. Anders visits a local centre where he often has lunch in the café. He enjoys the social and recreational activities organised by members. He has recently become a member of the older people's board who help to run the centre; they are busy organising a series of fund-raising events to develop a garden that can be used and be accessible to everyone.

In considering three brief examples of the provision of social care in three different countries you will have noted some similarities and differences. All three systems appear to focus on maintaining the older person, as far as possible, within their own home. The three countries have developed services – home care, day centres and so on – to support people in their own home and have opportunities for social and recreational facilities. In the USA and Germany there is a strong focus on the family, while in Denmark it is suggested that there is a stronger focus on independence from family. In the USA and Germany the focus is on cash through benefits and insurance; in Denmark there is a focus on developing services. All systems recognise the growing cost of providing care for older people. All of the social care systems are characterised by their individual circumstances in relation to their organisation, financing and service provision.

The position of older people can be considered historically (across time) and within their perceived place in society (spatially). The structuring of later adulthood can be seen across a range of dimensions – political structures and their response, economic factors, industry and urbanisation, gender divisions, family construction and obligations, issues of health, ideological constructions (the perception by society of older people) and professional responses.

Ageing can be a positive part of life if older people are socially active and occupy non-trivial roles linked to strong community boundaries and a clear social structure. In particular control by older people over information and resources (whether material or symbolic) is important.

C H A P T E R   S U M M A R Y

This chapter has focused on helping you to understand the position of older people in society and how the cultural, economic and social context of being an older person impacts upon and influences social work practice. In the first section of this chapter you considered the reasons for examining the position of older people in society and what may be the factors that optimise older people's experience of late adulthood. Through examining the historical context of the development of welfare services for older people, you were provided with the opportunity to see how this led to the development of current care services for older people – community care. You also examined the structural factors in society that influence the experience of older people. You considered how this could impact on the lives of older people and influence your practice. Finally you considered the development of welfare services in other countries in order to support you in placing the development of services for older people in England in a wider context.

FURTHER READING

Anttonen, A., Baldock, J. and Sipilä, J. (2003) *The Young, the Old and the State*. Cheltenham: Edward Elgar.
This book provides a comparative account of social services for children and older people in five key industrial nations – Finland, Germany, Japan, the United Kingdom and the United States – seeking to understand the development and qualities of welfare systems that are similar and those that are different.

Foote, C. and Stanners, C. (20002) *Integrated Care for Older People*. London: Jessica Kingsley.
This book explores the provision of multi-agency to services for older people using a systems approach. They illustrate how consultation and participation enable older people to be become equal partners in decision-making, reducing dependency and duplication of services.

Giarchi, G.G. (1996) *Caring for Older Europeans*. Aldershot: Arena.
Although a little dated, this book provides a good source of the various modes of care for older people throughout Europe.

Means, R., Morbey, H. and Smith, R. (2002) *From Community Care to Market Care?* Bristol: Policy Press.
This book provides a summary of the development of the welfare services from the 1970s, outlining contemporary concerns and debates in relation to key issues of practice such as the purchaser–provider split, the rationing of care and the health and social care divide.

WEBSITES

- **www.bmfsj.de**
- **www.detr.gov.uk**
- **www.europa.eu.int**
- **www.who.int/ageing**

Chapter 3

The legal and political context of social work with older people

The subject skills highlighted to demonstrate this knowledge in practice include:
3.2.2 Problem-solving skills
3.2.2.1 Managing problem-solving activities
3.2.2.2 Gathering information
3.2.2.3 Analysis and synthesis
3.2.2.4 Intervention and evaluation
5.2.1 Knowledge and understanding
• Ability to use this knowledge and understanding in work within specific practice contexts

Introduction

In this chapter you will examine the significance of legislative frameworks, policy directives and service delivery standards on social work practice with all older people.

As you work through the chapter you will look at some examples of key areas of legislation, guidance and standards that relate to social care services for older people. You will learn about the significance and potential implications of these documents for older people, service delivery and social work practice. The complex relationships between public, social and political philosophies, policies, priorities and the organisation and practice of social work will be integral to the discussions in this chapter.

It is not possible to provide detailed coverage of every piece of legislation, guidance and policy that may be relevant. However, the chapter aims to provide you with an overview of the legal and political context of social work practice with older people. You should also note that this chapter is not intended as a legal text, but rather as an introduction to how laws, national guidance, policies and standards impact upon everyday social work practice. Additionally, the examples and discussion in this chapter are based upon English statute and guidance; therefore if your interest is in the context of social work practice in other parts of the United Kingdom, you should supplement your reading with specifically relevant texts. Where legislation and guidance is discussed in depth in other chapters of this book, it will be referred to, but will not be explored in this chapter. For example, Chapter 6 focuses on the concepts of vulnerability, abuse, risks and rights in relation to social work practice with older people and looks in detail at *No Secrets: Guidance on developing and implementing multi-agency policies and procedures to protect vulnerable adults from abuse* (Department of Health, 2000a). Furthermore this chapter does not explore the legislation and guidance specifically addressing older people with mental ill health; for detailed information on this topic you should refer to Golightley (2004).

This chapter starts by introducing you to the broad legal and political context in which social work with older people is practised in our society today. You will then develop your understanding of some of the key components of the legal context of practice by looking briefly at the main types of laws and at some terminology, for example statutory instruments, regulations and codes of practice. Having explored the general legal and political context of social work practice and some of the key terms that will be used in the chapter, the main section of the chapter looks at some examples of significant national initiatives. This section is organised to reflect the main themes of the government's Modernisation Agenda. Within each of the subsections a selection of documents will be explored and you will be encouraged to develop your understanding of their impact on social work practice with older people through consideration of one case study that will be developed throughout the chapter. In the last subsection of this latter part of the chapter, you will look at how older people have been able to influence the development of social care services. The political voice of older people and their collective power will be referred to throughout the chapter, but it is in this section that, through the use of specific examples, the extent of older people's involvement and its impact upon services is critiqued. In this way you will be able to understand that, despite the necessary divisions within this chapter, in social work practice there exists a complex relationship between legislative requirements, the organisation and practice of social work and the needs and wishes of older people.

General legal and political context

In Chapter 2 you have considered the position of older people in society and the cultural, economic and social context of being an older person. In this introductory section of Chapter 3 you will increase your knowledge by reading about the significance of political and legal frameworks in setting the context of older people's lives. You will also look at how legislation, policy and the political background influence contemporary social work practice with older people.

The legislative framework related to health, social care and social welfare provision for older people in England and the resultant processes and services could be seen to have its origins in the work of William Beveridge in the development of social welfare in the period after the Second World War. However, to analyse the current environment we will consider the changes and drivers that are evident from more recent years. The early 1990s saw the implementation of the National Health Service and Community Care Act 1990 and the major reforms of community care services in England. These reforms reflected the Conservative government's political ideology at that time. The New Right philosophy of individual choice, the value of free-market competition and the merits of financial prudence and accountability can all be seen to have been motivators to change.

In 1997 a Labour government was elected and in 2001 it was re-elected with a substantial majority for a second term. The change in political stance of the government in power can be seen to have underpinned further developments in legislation and policy-making. Furthermore, following re-election, the growing confidence of the Labour government resulted in further, more rapid and more radical developments to the developing agenda in health and social care.

The foundation for many of these changes was set in a White Paper published early in this government's term of office, *Modernising Social Services: Promoting Independence, Improving Protection, Raising Standards* (DoH, 1998). Three other White Papers, each with the *modernisation* theme were also published at the end of the 1990s: *The New NHS: Modern, Dependable* (DoH, 1997), *Modern Local Government: In Touch with the People* (Deputy Prime Minister, 1998) and *Modernising Government* (Cabinet Office, 1999). The four White Papers have explicit and unambiguous links, and set out an ambitious plan for modernising all public services (Means et al., 2003: 74). It is to a great extent this modernisation agenda which can be seen to have laid out the political philosophies, policies and priorities that have directed the organisation and practice of social work with older adults in more recent years.

The modernisation agenda as outlined in these documents aims to improve the quality and effectiveness of public services, including social care, by tackling five broad areas:

- supporting independence, developing prevention strategies and services and promotion of well-being;

- protection of vulnerable people;

- improving standards and regulation, including staff development, organisational learning and training;

- equality of access to services across England;

- a partnership approach to working across the whole system, including participation of service users and the wider community.

You will consider each of these themes as you work through the chapter and will have the opportunity to learn how specific pieces of legislation, guidance and policy have been developed and implemented to support the overall modernisation agenda. Within this you will read about ways in which older people have been able to develop a political voice and how they have participated in service developments at different levels. In accordance with their stated political beliefs and the principles outlined in the White Papers, the current government have emphasised the status of older people as citizens. The term *citizenship* confers rights and responsibilities on an individual as a member of society, in particular the rights to participate and be involved in the community and in wider society (Audit Commission, 2004a).

All Our Tomorrows – Inverting the Triangle of Care

The Local Government Association (LGA) and the Association of Directors of Social Services (ADSS) commissioned a discussion paper to detail the progress and consider the future of health and social care services for older people. The following statements are extracts from the foreword to this document, written by David Behan, Alison King and Andrew Cozens, presidents of the association:

> *If we are to make real, significant and sustainable improvements in the quality of life of older people, we will need to take radical steps, rather than tinkering around the edges. Fundamental changes are needed in the way we think about ageing and older people. The way in which public services operate and are organised will need to be radically revised. The legislative underpinnings of services for older people need to be modernised to reflect a different vision for the future. We must do more to eradicate poverty and inequalities in health and well-being. The interface between the public sector and the private, voluntary and community sectors still needs to be improved and the value of informal carers better recognised ...*

> *The national aspirations for better services for older people are clear in the national service framework and the NHS plan and the new investments in health and social care reinforce this. The social services community is fully committed to the principles of opposing ageism, developing person-centred care, working in partnership with users and carers and the development of inclusive services. However, for local government, social services and the social care community and for the NHS, creating robust and responsive services which will meet the needs of today's and tomorrow's older people poses significant challenges and many new opportunities.*

(LGA, 2003: Foreword)

The quotations given in the box above are not only a useful summary to this section of the chapter, but should also make you think about whether the current legislative and policy frameworks are going to be effective in developing the types of services that older people would want to see in place. As you work through this chapter and look in more detail at some of the most significant national documents, think back to the statements above and consider whether these laws, policies and standards will assist social work practitioners to meet the *challenges and opportunities* of working with older people today and in the future.

Terminology

In order to help you to develop your understanding of the legal framework of practice with older people, this section will explain some key terms that are used in this context. This knowledge will ensure that you are able to recognise the implications, for older people and for social work practice, of the initiatives and documents referred to throughout the rest of the chapter.

In Table 3.1 below, some specific terms are listed with brief explanations and examples. However, there are other fundamental concepts that you need to understand in order to become familiar with the impact of national government programmes on social work practice and the lives of older adults.

Within the wealth of legislation, guidance and policy documents you will come across differing levels of permission or *powers*. These are most commonly referred to as *statutory* or *mandatory* powers and *discretionary* or *permissive* powers. The two are quite different although each describes a level of authorisation. *Statutory* or *mandatory* powers are those that *must* be carried out; there is no option or choice – statutory powers are non-negotiable. *Discretionary* or *permissive* powers, on the other hand, indicate what *can* or *may* be carried out; here there are options and possibilities as discretionary powers detail what an agency is allowed to do. The distinction between *must* and *can* is further reflected in the difference between *a power* and *a duty*, which are also terms you will find within legislative documentation.

Another distinction that you need to understand is that between statute law and common law. Statute law refers to legislation that has been debated and set by due political process and given royal assent as an Act of Parliament. Common law is more complex in that it relates to laws that are often constructed through common understandings and expectations in society, or have been established by the decisions of courts. Throughout this chapter you will learn about both statute laws and common laws that are highly influential to social work practice with older people.

Within the legal framework of social work practice a range of documents with different purposes and status help to support, interpret and develop the legislation. These documents operate in different ways, often having slightly different functions and status in the law. Table 3.1 defines some of the most frequently encountered documents. For further explanations on key terminology refer to Johns (2003) – see further reading.

Table 3.1 Defining key terms

	Description	Status
Statutory instrument	Sometimes known as *secondary legislation* as it details the procedures for how primary legislation or statute must be implemented. These are often schedules related to a specific Act of Parliament	Compulsory
Regulations or Directions	As with statutory instruments, these provide the detail, rules and procedures for putting an Act or part of an Act into practice	Compulsory
Guidance	Further interprets the law usually detailing how the government and ministers want the law to be understood	While not having the status of law, guidance must be followed unless there are valid and convincing reasons not to
Codes of practice	Detail models of good practice showing how Acts of Parliament should be implemented	Do not have the force of law
Circulars	Set out how legislation should be implemented but are often quite specific detailing, for example, financial arrangements or processes for inter-agency working	Do not have the force of law

The documents and national initiatives that are examined in this chapter set some of the legal requirements and guidance for social work practice with older adults. For the most part, such national directions need to be interpreted into more local and agency-specific policies and procedures. In this way political philosophies and policies that have driven national priorities are given meaning and put into a local context and, through local agreements and procedures will directly influence the actual daily practice of social workers working with older adults.

ACTIVITY 3.1

For this activity you will need to look at a local policy document. You could access this through the Internet or your local library or by directly contacting your local authority. The following are suggestions of local public access documents that you should be able to obtain easily, although you may find that the titles vary according to local decisions:

- *social services eligibility criteria for services;*

- *a policy on the protection of vulnerable adults;*

- *a policy or procedure in respect of access to direct payments.*

Then consider the following:

- *Look through one of the local policy documents suggested above.*

- *Which national initiative or priority is being implemented through this document?*

- *In what ways have the national requirements been reflected in the local document?*

The first point to note is whether you found this information easy to obtain. We would hope that this was a straightforward activity; however, if you had difficulty finding the documents you can assume that access would be equally difficult for older people who might want to enquire about relevant services. In terms of these specific documents, eligibility criteria should reflect the national requirement for *Fair Access to Care Services*, which you will read more about later in this chapter; policies on the protection of vulnerable adults should reflect the national *No Secrets* document, which is examined in Chapter 6 of this book; local information about direct payments should show how the various pieces of legislation and guidance on the provision of direct payments are being implemented locally.

Key legal and policy documents

In this chapter so far, you have read an overview of the legal and political context of social work practice with older people and have developed your knowledge in terms of the status of different national documents and directives. In this main section of the chapter you will focus on some specific examples of national documents and explore the implications for social work practice with older people. You will study legislation and guidance that is particularly relevant to this area of social work using headings informed by the themes of the *modernisation agenda* discussed earlier in this chapter: supporting independence, developing prevention strategies and services, promotion of well-being and protection of vulnerable people; improving standards and regulation; citizenship and equality of access to services; partnership and participation. Of course, in social work practice it is not possible to separate these areas in this way. In reality there are intricate interrelationships, between these documents, that set the context, complexity, challenges and dilemmas that are inherent in professional social work practice. To assist you to recognise these issues, the following case study will be referred to throughout this section.

CASE STUDY

Sarah and Robert Daniels have been married for 39 years and live in a town about 25 miles from Southampton. Sarah is 68 years old, Robert is 73 years old. They have two children who are both married and live in Southampton. Sarah and Robert retired from full-time work a few months ago. For the past 22 years they have owned and run an independent general store in the town, living in the flat above the shop. The Danielses have now sold the business and the premises, but with an arrangement that they can continue living in their flat as tenants of the new owners.

This gives you an outline of the case study situation, which will be developed as you study the following sections of the chapter.

Supporting independence, developing prevention strategies and services, promotion of well-being and protection of vulnerable people

The modernisation agenda outlined earlier in the chapter can be traced back to the latter part of the 1990s. The priorities of this approach, particularly the emphasis given to increasing independence, preventative strategies and the protection of vulnerable people, have frequently been implemented through guidance and circulars that add to or update core statutes. For example, you will firstly consider the National Health Service and Community Care Act 1990 (NHS and CCA), which received royal assent before the first Labour government modernisation reforms were announced. However, the more recent policy guidance, produced as a Local Authority Circular, *Fair Access to Care Services* (DoH, 2002), provides a mandatory framework for developing eligibility criteria for adult social care services that acknowledges the need for services that will promote independence. This guidance develops and is underpinned by section 47 of the National Health Service and Community Care Act 1990 which states that local authorities 'shall then decide whether his needs call for the provision of any such services' (NHS and CCA 1990, s.47(1)(b)). It can, therefore, be seen that the commitment to reform has sometimes changed the original emphasis to bring it into harmony with the modernisation principles. In respect of the example above, the original act prioritised services for those individuals deemed to be 'in greatest need', yet subsequent directives, in the *Fair Access to Care Services* circular and others, have shifted the emphasis to preventative services that will promote and maintain the independence of individuals who may have lower levels of need at that time.

National Health Service and Community Care Act 1990

The National Health Service and Community Care Act 1990 (NHS and CCA) was fully implemented in April 1993. This legislation was developed and put in place following much political and social debate. The Griffiths Report (Griffiths, 1988) set out the key issues and recommendations that were largely reflected in the White Paper *Caring for People: Community Care in the next Decade and Beyond* (DoH, 1989). Subsequently, the Act brought about major changes in how community care services are provided and arranged at individual, management and strategic levels. However, this legislation did not supersede other pieces of legislation, but was supplementary to pre-existing laws, for example the National Assistance Act 1948 and the Mental Health Act 1983. Additionally, the NHS and CCA was supplemented by practice guidance that details the processes, procedures and practices required by practitioners and managers to implement the Act (DoH, 1990a, 1991).

One of the changes brought about by this legislation that may have been initially the most noticeable not only to professionals working in community care services but also to older people and their families was the change to funding arrangements for residential and nursing care provision in the independent sector. Prior to April 1993, people entering this form of care could do so via the benefit system, through an application for higher levels of income support to fund the care. There was no requirement for assessment or planning to meet their care needs and no process of identification of the most appropriate form of care to meet those needs. The NHS and CCA transformed this system, requiring all applicants who would need assistance with funding their care to go through the local authority and the processes laid down in the legislation. Hence it could be argued that the most significant statutory duties that arise from this Act are the duty to assess needs and the duty to arrange social care in the public and the independent sector. Other key sections of the act are summarised in the box below.

National Health Service and Community Care Act 1990

The Act provides definitions of *community care services* as those services that are provided under other pre-existing legislation:

- Part III National Assistance Act 1948 (residential and welfare services);
- section 45, Health Services and Public Health Act 1968 (welfare of elderly people);
- section 21, Schedule 8, National Health Service Act 1977 (home help);
- section 117, Mental Health Act 1983 (after-care services).

The following sections of the NHS and CCA are the most commonly referred to in the provision of social care services for older people:

- *section 42* – permits local authorities to make arrangements for nursing home care in private and voluntary homes;
- *section 44* – addresses charging policies and requires local authorities to determine a *standard rate* for accommodation arranged by them;

▶

- *section 46* – establishes a duty for local authorities to prepare and publish community care plans in consultation with other local agencies, including health and housing. This section of the Act also provides a definition of *community care*;

- *section 47* – sets out a statutory duty for local authorities to assess the needs and plan for individual care;

- *section 48* – requires the establishment of inspection units separate from Social Services to inspect and report upon local authority and registered residential independent care homes;

- *section 50* – requires local authorities to establish a procedure for considering any representations (including complaints) made to them.

The most prominent areas of change in this legislation and its original supporting guidance documents can be grouped into three main themes, as follows.

The development of care management and assessment

The 1989 White Paper (DoH, 1989: 5) stressed that a primary objective of the community care reforms was 'to make proper assessment of need and good case management the cornerstone of high quality care' (Means et al., 2003). This objective was to be met through a range of measures including the separation of assessment and the purchasing of services from the provision of those services. The assessment and commissioning of social care services would be a *care management* function. Furthermore, assessments for community care services – *community care assessments* – should take a *needs-led approach*, which the Department of Health describes as 'the process of tailoring services to individual needs' (DoH, 1990a: 11). The practice guidance states that assessment is only one part of the care management process that consists of seven *core tasks*:

Stage One	Publishing information
Stage Two	Determining the level of assessment
Stage Three	Assessing need
Stage Four	Care planning
Stage Five	Implementing the care plan
Stage Six	Monitoring
Stage Seven	Reviewing

Stages Four and Five of the process are also significant in that *care planning* and *implementing the care plan* also require consideration of what services can or will be provided. The aim of this legislation and subsequent guidance was to make the services which are arranged following assessment more effective, responsive and accountable. However, you should consider these issues and reflect upon whether the notion of a needs-led approach and targeting services through local authority-determined eligibility criteria are compatible.

The development of a mixed economy of care provision

The NHS and CCA, as stated earlier, reformed the way care was funded and arrang extended local authorities' powers to enable them to purchase services from the pr and voluntary sector. In fact, through additional requirements linked to funding arran ments, local authorities were required to spend high proportions of the specified budget in this sector, thus competition between providers was encouraged, the statutory sector was no longer to be the main direct provider of services and the *mixed economy of care* was promoted. Local authorities were charged with encouraging the growth of a range of services in their community, promoting user choice and enabling these services to be supplied by other organisations. Following the theme of being needs-led, services were to be developed to meet individual needs through individual care planning that would detail the required outcomes.

Additionally, the aspiration that services should further independence, responding flexibly and appropriately to individual need, became a driving force in the notion of encouraging the increase in provision of services in the community and the reduction of residential-type services. However, increasingly the high cost of providing domiciliary services into individual older people's homes has led to local authorities applying financial cost ceilings. This means that where the provision of home care services becomes more expensive than provision of residential care to meet the same identified needs, the cheaper option is the only option available to that service-user. While this is contrary, not only to the principles of the modernisation agenda and the government's stated strategies, but also to the values and ethics of social work practice and often the wishes of individual older people, residential care services are defined as community care services and therefore, in terms of the law, this action is permissible (Johns, 2003: 86). Furthermore, in respect of developing the care provision market, such actions and decisions by the main service purchaser could be seen to constrain free-market forces. In this example, any financial ceiling on the purchase of domiciliary services may inhibit the growth of services in that sector. The opposing argument, however, would stress the potential benefits of keeping costs down and possibly increasing competitiveness in the market.

The development of partnerships

Within the Act and the various guidance documents to the Act, there are explicit references to working with others. Firstly the Act emphasises the importance of working with service users and carers making certain that their views are influential and choices are increased. Services should consider the need for representation and advocacy for service users ensuring greater accountability to older people and their carers for service quality and effectiveness. However, Means et al. (2003: 67) cite research undertaken by Hardy et al. (1999) in four local authorities which suggests that in reality the amount of choice available is very limited.

The requirement for joint working and collaboration across agencies is also integral to this legislation which states, for example, that local authorities *shall consult* with other authorities, namely health, housing and voluntary organisations, in the development of community care plans. Furthermore, in assessing individual needs for community care services, authorities are required to *notify* other agencies and *take account* of their services, as appropriate, when assessing and deciding about services. This aims to develop integrated and co-ordinated services between the different agencies.

Figure 3.1 summarises the key themes of this Act. As the NHS & CCA is a central element of the legal framework for social work with older people, we have dedicated a considerable section of this chapter to exploring the most significant elements of it. However, there are still many areas of this legislation that we have not been able to cover and we therefore recommend that you take your studies further by looking at the recommended reading and Internet resources offered at the end of the chapter.

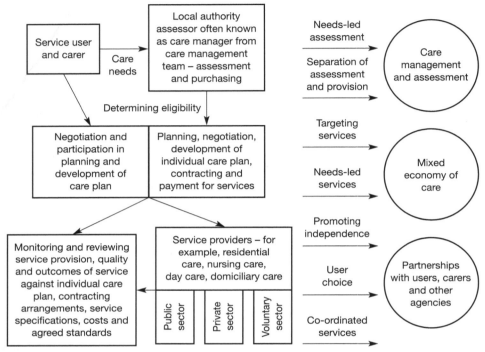

Figure 3.1 *National Health Service and Community Care Act 1990 – main themes of the legislation and guidance*

Direct payments

One of the aims embedded within the NHS and CCA, as you have seen, was to increase service user choice. However, at the same time the potentially conflicting principals of targeting services to those in greatest need (DoH, 1990b) and the development of local eligibility criteria for services could be seen to restrict options available to older people. The Community Care (Direct Payments) Act 1996 set out to address the issues of choice and control over services by giving local authorities the power to provide cash payments to certain individuals to enable them to arrange and purchase their own care services. This legislation was implemented in 1997 with accompanying regulations excluding people over the age of 65 years from direct payments unless they started to receive the payments before their 65th birthday. You should note that this legislation gave local authorities the *power* to make direct payments; it was not a duty for them to do so.

In 2000 through Statutory Instrument 2000/11 direct payments were extended to people over the age of 65 years. Further policy and practice guidance (DoH, 2000b) signified the government's aim to 'increase the availability of direct payments and to ensure that particular groups of service users were not excluded' (Glasby and Littlechild, 2002: 42). The guidance encourages authorities to extend the use of the scheme and directs them to look at each situation on a case-by-case basis. Further legislative change came with the implementation of the Carers and Disabled Children Act 2000, which extended direct payments to carers. This has been followed by further regulations which replace and update elements of previous legislation and guidance, placing a *duty* upon local authorities to offer direct payments to people who meet the criteria and wish to take up the option (DoH, 2003). In order to further boost the development of direct payments, in future the government will be measuring local authorities' performance on this issue. The method of making this measure and some of the results are shown in the box below.

Social Services Performance Assessment Framework Indicator – Direct Payments AO/C51

- Adults and older people receiving direct payments at 31 March 2003 per 100,000 population aged 18 or over (age standardised).

- In England the average for 2002/3 was 23 people receiving direct payments per 100,000 population aged 18 or over. As at 20 September 2002, 1,032 older people in England were in receipt of direct payments.

Source: **www.publications.doh.gov.uk/paf**

As you have seen the development of direct payments has taken place over many years with older people only being included in the schemes from 2000. Below is a summary of the main features of direct payments legislation and guidance that will impact upon your work with older people.

What are the payments to be used for?
- The payments are used to purchase services to provide care to meet the assessed needs of the individual.

- Direct payments can be used to purchase residential care, but only for a maximum of four weeks in any 12-month period.

- Direct payments can be used to pay for the services of a close relative or spouse, at the discretion of the local authority who should satisfy themselves that this is necessary to meet the individual's needs for that service. (Prior to the 2003 regulations the employment of close relatives, using direct payments, was prohibited.)

- Direct payments cannot be used to purchase services that are provided by the local authority and they cannot be used to purchase healthcare.

- If the service user does not spend the money on services to meet the assessed needs, the local authority has the right to cease payments. However, the authority would then be responsible for ensuring that they arranged services to meet the person's needs in another way.

Who is eligible for payments?

- The service user must be willing and able to manage the direct payment themselves or with assistance.

How much money can be paid to individual people under direct payments?

- The amount of money paid would depend upon the assessment of care needs for that individual and the cost of providing that care in an alternative way.

- Any payment would be net of the usual charges for services made by the local authority.

Direct payment schemes could be criticised for being too cumbersome and complex. There are many practical tasks that any potential direct payments user needs to consider, including: managing the accounts, which must be auditable; employment issues such as the recruitment of, legislation covering and payment of income tax and national insurance for any care staff employed; and responsibilities in terms of health and safety. However, despite these potential difficulties, with appropriate support and guidance direct payments can be liberating, allowing people to regain control and power in their lives. You should note, though, that even where a user is in receipt of a direct payment from the local authority, that authority remains responsible, under the legislation, to assess and develop the agreed care plan, and to review and monitor the individual's care needs and services.

In recent government guidance the Department of Health acknowledges that it is looking to extend the usage of direct payments.

> For that reason, local councils now have not just a power, but a duty to make direct payments in certain circumstances. This has important implications for the way that local councils undertake assessment and care planning discussions with individuals, and for local councils' own commissioning procedures and planning. For some staff/professionals, direct payments may require a significant change from current ways of working with people needing services. However, those staff who have made the 'cultural leap' have discovered that they experience the great satisfaction that comes from expanding individuals' lifestyle choices. (DoH, 2003: 5)

Glasby and Littlechild (2002) discuss how social work practice needs to develop in order to assist and support older people to explore the options offered by direct payments. They stress the importance of social workers making sure that they keep themselves up to date with relevant knowledge and that this is passed on to service users and carers in an accessible way.

> Time and time again, a major barrier to an extension of direct payments has been shown to be the anxiety and ignorance of frontline social workers. (Glasby and Littlechild, 2002: 105)

> It is our firm belief that direct payments offer practitioners a new and extremely exciting way of working, empowering service users to be more in control of their own lives. Whether or not individual social workers are prepared to accept this challenge is ultimately down to them. (Glasby and Littlechild, 2002: 138)

50

Legislation and guidance to support carers

The definition of a carer is provided within the Carers (Recognition and Services) Act 1995 as 'someone who provides a substantial amount of care on a regular basis to another'. Definitions of *substantial* and *regular* are not offered, but it is clear that the carer must not be providing that care under a contract of employment or as a volunteer for a voluntary organisation. Therefore the discussion below refers to family, friends and neighbours of older people, whom we shall call informal carers.

The legal context of work to support informal carers, in keeping with other initiatives that you have seen throughout this chapter, has increasingly been developed within the underlying principles of the modernisation agenda: supporting independence, developing prevention strategies and services, promotion of well-being and protection of vulnerable people. Over recent years there has been increasing recognition of the importance of carers in providing substantial levels of care and support that is often not acknowledged or even known about. This recognition is reflected in the abundance of legislation and guidance that now exists to support their role. In addition to specific statutes, guidance and strategies, the needs of carers have been embedded within the National Service Framework for Older People (DoH, 2001a) and the National Service Framework for Mental Health (DoH, 1999a).

The Carers (Recognition and Services) Act 1995

This was the first piece of legislation to directly address the needs and rights of informal carers. This Act gives carers, who provide *substantial and regular care*, the right to ask for an assessment of their own needs as part of the assessment undertaken of the cared for person. This led to the development of carer's assessment policies and procedures within local social services agencies.

Carers National Strategy

This strategy document entitled *Caring about Carers* (DoH, 1999b) draws attention to the need for legislation that will allow for services to be provided directly to meet the needs of carers, the government's stated aim being to support carers, not only to continue their caring role, but also to protect their own health and well-being. The strategy has four main themes that specifically affect the carers of older people:

1. Information for carers – to enable meaningful partnerships.

2. Support for carers – from the community to plan and provide services.

3. Care for carers – to maintain their own health and independence.

4. Carers and employment – enabling and encouraging carers to remain in work.

(Audit Commission, 2004b)

Carers and Disabled Children Act 2000

The Carers and Disabled Children Act 2000 was implemented in April 2001. This statute delivers many of the proposals first seen in the *Carers National Strategy*, for example the Act gives local authorities the power to supply services direct to carers in their own right, following an appropriate assessment. The Act is clear that the assessment and resultant services are not dependent upon the needs or wishes of the cared for person. The Act, as is implied by its title, also addresses the needs of those who care for a disabled child.

In respect of carers of older people this Act is significant in that it enshrines not only their rights to an assessment, but also to services that will support them as carers or will promote their own continued independence. The Act also enables authorities to consider alternative ways to provide services to carers, through direct payments to carers to purchase services to meet their own assessed needs and through the provision of short-term break voucher schemes.

In this section you have looked at the NHS and CCA 1990 and legislation to implement direct payments to support informal carers. These are key examples of legislation and policy that support older people's independence and promote their well-being. The following activity, using the case study introduced earlier, will enable you to consider how these initiatives affect social work practice.

ACTIVITY 3.2

Sarah and Robert Daniels are retired shop owners. Sarah is 68 years old and Robert is 73 years old, and they have always prided themselves on their good health and active lifestyle. However, only a few months after retiring, Robert was taken suddenly very ill and, following a visit by his General Practitioner, he was admitted to hospital. After initial tests, the hospital doctors diagnosed that Robert had had a cerebral vascular accident (CVA), commonly known as a stroke. After a range of treatments given over a period of weeks in hospital, the medical team inform Robert and Sarah that he is ready for discharge, as he has reached the stage where hospital treatment is no longer necessary. However, Robert and Sarah are surprised and anxious about this, as Robert remains considerably physically disabled from the stroke. Sarah is exhausted by the frequent hospital visits and is very apprehensive about what the future may hold. However, Robert and Sarah agree that if he is to be discharged, then he should go straight back to the flat above the shop where they live.

Having read the case study of Sarah and Robert Daniels, write down your thoughts on the following:

- *How does the NHS and CCA 1990 and subsequent practitioner guidance inform the process and practice that will happen now?*

- *Do you think that Robert could be entitled to receive a direct payment and, if so, what do you base this on?*

- *What does the legislation and guidance related to social work practice with informal carers tell us about how Sarah should be supported in the caring role?*

By referring back to the section covering the NHS and CCA 1990 you will be reminded of how this sets out core tasks in the process of care management that includes the provision of information followed by an appropriate level of assessment of need. It is likely that this process actually started near the beginning of Robert's hospital admission, so that information will have been provided and the assessment of need, using the single assessment process within an interprofessional framework, would have commenced. Within this process direct payments should be discussed with Robert and Sarah. Robert will meet the criteria for direct payments as he is able to manage the process; however, it will depend upon his needs assessment and the types of services that he wishes to purchase. Additionally, following implementation of the Carers and Disabled Children Act 2000, Sarah may be entitled to direct payments in her own right as a carer to support her in caring for Robert and to ensure that her own health and independence is maintained. Furthermore, in terms of support as an informal carer of an older person, Sarah is entitled to an assessment of her needs, which may lead to services being provided to support her directly.

Improving standards and regulation

Throughout the government's modernisation agenda the drive to improve standards and increase accountability through regulation and measurement is explicit. These themes were particularly apparent in the objectives and proposals laid out in *A Quality Strategy for Social Care* (DoH, 2000c), which detailed plans to reform social care training and practice. The desire to improve standards and consistency is also evident within *The NHS Plan 2000* (DoH, 2000d) where the notion of national service frameworks, or standards, is introduced. You will find more information about *The NHS Plan 2000* (DoH, 2000d) later in the chapter. In this section we have selected two documents that are particularly relevant to social work practice with older people: the Care Standards Act 2000 through which you will be able to increase your knowledge about workforce development and regulation, and *The National Service Framework for Older People* (DoH, 2001a) which is specifically about the standards of health and social care services for older adults.

Care Standards Act 2000

The Care Standards Act 2000 reformed the regulatory systems for social care services in England and Wales. The main aspects of this legislation that impact upon social work with older people are given below:

- The Act established the National Care Standards Commission (NCSC). This is a new, independent regulatory body for social care and private and voluntary healthcare services in England.

- The Act established the General Social Care Council (GSCC). This independent Council sets standards and codes of practice for social care work, registers social care workers and regulates the education and training of social workers.

- The Act provides for the establishment and maintenance of a list of individuals who are considered unsuitable to work with vulnerable adults. This is explored further in Chapter 6.

Source: **www.hmso.gov.uk/acts/en/2000**

The first two of these aspects and how they affect social care services with older people are considered below.

The National Care Standards Commission

The NCSC was required, by the Act, to register and regulate a vast range of care services. This includes the regulation of services that older people may access, such as domiciliary care agencies, all care homes, and private and voluntary healthcare services. This was a new requirement for domiciliary services and also, for the first time, local authorities were required to meet the same standards as independent sector providers.

Since the implementation of the Care Standards Act, further changes to the structure of the regulatory bodies have been made. From April 2004, the NCSC was replaced by two new inspectorates, the Commission for Social Care Inspection (CSCI) and the Health Care Commission. The Commission for Social Care Inspection is responsible for a range of registration and inspection functions including work previously carried out by the Social Services Inspectorate (SSI) and the SSI/Audit Commission joint review work, as well as the social care activities of the NCSC as described above. For further information you should explore their website at **www.csci.org.uk**.

The General Social Care Council

The GSCC is required to register and regulate the social care workforce. The GSCC has a duty to promote high standards of conduct and practice in the profession, which includes the setting of standards for and regulation in respect of social work training. Through the Social Care Register, the GSCC aims to ensure that all social workers and social care workers are suitable for work with vulnerable people. In order to register, individuals will have to meet a range of criteria; they are also required to demonstrate agreement with, compliance with and commitment to the Codes of Practice for social care workers. The Codes of Practice include standards for social care employers and standards for social care workers. An extract from the Codes of Practice for social care workers is given in the box below – for further information you should explore the GSCC website at **www.gscc.org.uk**.

General Social Care Council Code of Practice for Social Care Workers and Employers

The purpose of this code is to set out the conduct that is expected of social care workers and to inform service users and the public about the standards of conduct they can expect from such workers. It forms part of the wider package of legislation, practice standards and employers' policies and procedures that social care workers must meet. Social care workers are responsible for making sure that their conduct does not fall below the standards set out in this code and that no action or omission on their part harms the well-being of service users.

Social care workers must:

- protect the rights and promote the interests of service users and carers;

- strive to establish and maintain the trust and confidence of service users and carers;

- promote the independence of service users while protecting them as far as possible from danger or harm;

- respect the rights of service users while seeking to ensure that their behaviour does not harm themselves or other people;

- uphold public trust and confidence in social care services; and

- be accountable for the quality of their work and take responsibility for maintaining and improving their knowledge and skills.

Source: GSCC (2002)

You will have the opportunity to explore the Care Standards Act 2000 further in chapter 6 where the protection of vulnerable older people is discussed.

National Service Framework for Older People

The NHS Plan (DoH, 2000d) introduced the concept of National Service Frameworks (NSFs) which have been published on a rolling programme. For example, there are now established frameworks on mental health, cancer services, coronary heart disease, diabetes and older people. These frameworks set national standards and outline models of service and expected levels of performance. They are written and organised so that multi-disciplinary and multi-agency working is integral (Statham, 2004). The NSF for Older People was published in 2001 and has become a substantial influence on the development and direction of health and social care services for older people. Figure 3.2 illustrates how the overall aims of the NSF for Older People and the key themes of the *modernisation agenda* correspond to work together to inform and support each strategy. In Chapters 6 and 7 of this book, you will have another opportunity to increase your understanding of the significance of specific elements of the standards for particular areas of social work practice with older people.

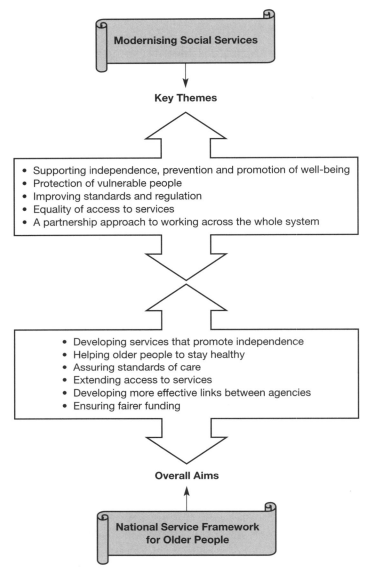

Figure 3.2 *Themes of the modernisation agenda and aims of the NSF for Older People*

Given their importance for contemporary social work with older people, we have outlined each of the standards in the box below.

National Service Framework for Older People (DoH, 2001a)

Standard 1: Rooting out age discrimination
Aim – To ensure that older people are never unfairly discriminated against in accessing NHS or social care services as a result of their age.

Standard – NHS services will be provided, regardless of age, on the basis of clinical need alone. Social care services will not use age in their eligibility criteria or policies to restrict access to available services.

Standard 2: Person-centred care
Aim – To ensure that older people are treated as individuals and they receive appropriate and timely packages of care which meet their needs as individuals, regardless of health and social services boundaries.

Standard – NHS and social care services treat older people as individuals and enable them to make choices about their own care. This is achieved through the single assessment process, integrated commissioning arrangements and integrated provision of services, including community equipment and continence services.

Standard 3: Intermediate care
Aim – To provide integrated services to promote faster recovery from illness, to prevent unnecessary acute hospital admissions, to support timely discharge and to maximise independent living.

Standard – Older people will have access to a new range of intermediate care services at home or in designated care settings to promote their independence by providing enhanced services from the NHS and councils to prevent unnecessary hospital admission and effective rehabilitation services to enable early discharge from hospital and to prevent premature or unnecessary admission to long-term residential care.

Standard 4: General hospital care
Aim – To ensure that older people receive the specialist help they need in hospital and that they receive the maximum benefit from having been in hospital.

Standard – Older people's care in hospital is delivered through appropriate specialist care and by hospital staff who have the right set of skills to meet their needs.

Standard 5: Stroke
Aim – To reduce the incidence of stroke in the population and ensure that those who have had a stroke have prompt access to integrated stroke care services.

Standard – The NHS will take action to prevent strokes, working in partnership with other agencies where appropriate. People who are thought to have had a stroke have access to diagnostic services, are treated appropriately by a specialist stroke service, and subsequently, with their carers, participate in a multi-disciplinary programme of secondary prevention and rehabilitation.

Standard 6: Falls

Aim – To reduce the number of falls which result in serious injury and ensure effective treatment and rehabilitation for those who have fallen.

Standard – The NHS, working in partnership with councils, takes action to prevent falls and reduce resultant fractures or other injuries in their populations of older people. Older people who have fallen receive effective treatment and rehabilitation and, with their carers, receive advice on prevention through a specialised falls service.

Standard 7: Mental health in older people

Aim – To promote good mental health in older people and to treat and support those older people with dementia and depression.

Standard – Older people who have mental health problems have access to integrated mental health services provided by the NHS and councils to ensure effective diagnosis, treatment and support, for them and for their carers.

Standard 8: Promoting an active, healthy life

Aim – to extend the healthy life expectancy of older people.

Standard – The health and well-being of older people is promoted through a co-ordinated programme of action led by the NHS with support from councils.

Source: DoH (2001a)

The information above provides you with an outline of each of the standards in the NSF for Older People. You will find it useful to examine the whole document, or the summary document in more detail, as this includes information such as the rationale behind each standard and the expected service models to deliver the requirements.

We have included the framework in this section of the chapter because this document is clearly about setting national standards to improve quality and consistency of services for older adults. However, you may have also recognised, within the standards, the cross-cutting themes from the modernisation agenda that formed the heading for the previous section of this chapter. Standards 3 and 8 are explicit about supporting independence, Standards 3, 5, 6, 7 and 8 are all related to developing and improving preventative services, while Standard 8 specifically focuses on the promotion of health and well-being. Furthermore, you should note the emphasis on partnership and participation, which is a theme that we develop later in the chapter.

In this section you have read about two examples of national initiatives that support the modernisation agenda principle of enhancing standards and regulation: the Care Standards Act 2000 and the NSF for Older People. The following activity asks you to consider how these might apply in social work practice situations.

Sarah and Robert have to make decisions about their future following Robert's admission to hospital after having a stroke. Robert remains considerably physically disabled from the stroke and unable to attend to his personal care needs without help. His mobility is also very restricted. However, he no longer requires hospital treatment and following the completion of a single assessment, the multi-disciplinary team have agreed that Robert should be discharged. The assessment has shown, though, that Robert is still in the early stages of recovery from the stroke and that he may be able to develop further independence skills over a period of time. Robert and Sarah are determined that he will come back to live in their first-floor flat, so that they may continue to enjoy their retirement together.

As you can see, the Sarah and Robert Daniels' situation has progressed. Consider the questions below and write down your responses.

- *How will the National Service Framework for Older People standards influence the services that Robert and Sarah may receive now? Are there some standards that might be more relevant than others?*

- *In what way might the requirements of the Care Standards Act 2000 impact upon the process and practices that will happen now?*

We would suggest that all the standards are relevant to Robert's situation and potential care needs. However, the three standards that might be considered particularly significant are Standard 2: Person-centred care, Standard 3: Intermediate care and Standard 5: Stroke. You will learn about Standard 2 in Chapter 7 of this book, in respect of the single assessment process. We shall consider briefly here how intermediate care services and stroke care services might be beneficial in Robert's situation.

Intermediate care service arrangements will differ around the country but will always meet the NSF standard by encompassing certain fundamental features. Rehabilitation from acute hospital care to independence at home and/or an approach that prevents admission to hospital and maximises independent living is the main function of intermediate care services. The NSF refers to services that 'bridge the gap' (DoH, 2001: 41) – these are usually intensive, short-term, time-limited interventions. Additionally, services will involve inter-professional working, usually within a multi-agency team, although the setting for care provision may vary. So, for the case study scenario, where Robert does not need medical or hospital care but remains considerably dependent upon help from other people, a short intensive period of intermediate care may be appropriate. This would depend upon the outcome of the single assessment, which would incorporate Robert and Sarah's views and the perspective of all the relevant professionals.

Standard 5 of the NSF for Older People is specifically about the development of integrated stroke care services. These services will work in conjunction with intermediate care services as, again, early and continuing rehabilitation are a feature, alongside an inter-professional approach that enables holistic and comprehensive care regardless of whether that care is received in hospital, at home or in any other setting. For Robert's situation, continued rehabilitation specific to his assessed needs is now important and this may be received from a special stroke care service or through an intermediate care service.

Robert and Sarah should be assured that, due to the requirements of the Care Standards Act 2000, any social care workers that come into their home will work to a common set of standards and values. They can be confident in service providers who will be regulated, registered, monitored and inspected through the CSCI. The Commission could also provide information to Robert and Sarah on suitably registered providers. Additionally, through the requirements of the NHS and CCA, examined earlier, Robert and Sarah will have redress to a local authority social services complaints procedure, should they have concerns about the quality of care provided.

Equality of access to services

The themes of equality of opportunity and access to services are threaded throughout the legislation, guidance and policy documents that you are exploring in this chapter. In this section, as one particular example, you will develop your understanding of the *Fair Access to Care Services* guidance (DoH, 2002), which has been briefly discussed earlier, as this is particularly important to older people accessing social care services.

There are other areas of legislation which raise equality issues for older people that we are not able to cover in this chapter. The Human Rights Act 1998 is discussed in Chapter 6 along with the draft Mental Incapacity Bill (2003). You could also extend your studies further by finding out about the implications for older adults of the Race Relations Amendment Act 2000 and the EU employment directive on equal treatment (you will find information about this directive and the government's response at **www.dwp.gov.uk**) due to be introduced in 2006.

Fair Access to Care Services (FACS): Guidance on Eligibility Criteria for Adult Social Care

This policy guidance was published in 2002 as a Local Authority Circular LAC (2002) 13. The guidance provides local authorities with an eligibility framework for setting and applying their local criteria for adult social care. FACS was implemented in April 2003, with the aim of ensuring fairer and more consistent eligibility decisions across the country. The full guidance and the circular can be found on **www.doh.gov.uk/scg/facs**.

It is important to note that this is about eligibility to have needs met, not eligibility to have needs assessed. The framework has four eligibility bands or categories, which focus on the individual's needs and associated risks to independence. The Department of Health has stressed that when applying the criteria, staff should consider all the needs of the individual, including current needs and potential needs should services not be put in place. However, the local authority has the discretion to decide their local threshold on a reviewable basis. Those individuals assessed as falling into bands above the threshold must have their needs met, those falling below the threshold will not be eligible for a service. This threshold decision can be made with due regard to the authority's financial resources; however, within the implementation of the criteria there is no link to cost.

Another principle of this guidance is that each authority will only have one set of ⌐
through which judgments about all adult care needs will be made. So, regardless of aɣ
type of care need, illness or disability, or potential service provision, one set of eligibility
criteria will be used.

Fair Access to Care Services (FACS): Guidance on Eligibility Criteria for Adult Social Care

Critical – is when

- Life is, or will be threatened; and/or

- Significant health problems have developed or will develop; and/or

- There is, or will be, little or no choice and control over vital aspects of the immediate environment; and/or

- Serious abuse or neglect has occurred or will occur; and/or

- There is, or will be, an inability to carry out vital personal care or domestic routines; and/or

- Vital involvement in work, education or learning cannot or will not be sustained; and/or

- Vital social support systems and relationships cannot or will not be sustained; and/or

- Vital family and other social roles and responsibilities cannot or will not be undertaken.

Substantial – is when

- There is, or will be, only partial choice and control over the immediate environment; and/or

- Abuse or neglect has occurred or will occur; and/or

- There is, or will be, an inability to carry out the majority of personal care or domestic routines; and/or

- Involvement in many aspects of work, education or learning cannot or will not be sustained; and/or

- The majority of social support systems and relationships cannot or will not be sustained; and/or

- The majority of family and other social roles and responsibilities cannot or will not be undertaken.

Moderate – is when

- There is, or will be, an inability to carry out several personal care or domestic routines; and/or

- Involvement in several aspects of work, education or learning cannot or will not be sustained; and/or

- Several social support systems and relationships cannot or will not be sustained; and/or

- Several family and other social roles and responsibilities cannot or will not be undertaken.

Low – is when

- There is, or will be, an inability to carry out one or two personal care or domestic routines; and/or

- Involvement in one or two aspects of work, education or learning cannot or will not be sustained; and/or

- One or two social support systems and relationships cannot or will not be sustained; and/or

- One or two family and other social roles and responsibilities cannot or will not be undertaken.

Source: (DoH, 2002)

Means et al. (2003) make the point that the publication of this framework is only a starting point. Substantial longer-term monitoring, evaluation and research into its implementation across the nation and its impact upon older adults have yet to be undertaken.

In this chapter you have only been given an introduction to this guidance as the full document goes beyond eligibility criteria alone. It also provides direction on risk assessment, commissioning services, care planning and reviewing. Furthermore, the FACS guidance and its local implementation must also be seen alongside joint eligibility for continuing health and social care services, which are provided under section 31 of the Health Act 1999. This is discussed further in the next section of this chapter.

ACTIVITY **3.4**

Look back at the case study of Robert and Sarah. Read the developments below:

Sarah and Robert have to consider longer-term services following Robert's discharge from hospital after treatment for a stroke. Robert was discharged from hospital six weeks ago and has been living with his wife at home in their first-floor flat. Over the past six weeks Robert has received an intensive level of services from an intermediate care team, including physiotherapy, district nursing support, occupational therapy, domiciliary care services and appropriate medical supervision. Robert and Sarah have been surprised and pleased with the level of improvement in Robert's abilities over the six-week period. Following a review meeting, it has been agreed that this service will be withdrawn. It is predicted that Robert's level of impairment will remain stable for the foreseeable future.

However, Robert is not fully independent. He can now manage most personal care tasks reasonably well but has considerable difficulty getting in and out of the flat. Adaptations and equipment have been provided following hospital discharge and these have enabled Robert to move around the flat independently. Sarah continues to provide the emotional support and encouragement that Robert needs; however, due to Robert's care needs, the couple are becoming increasingly isolated in their flat. Robert had retired only months before the stroke. For many years he owned and managed an independent general store. He is now becoming frustrated and bored with inactivity and would like to have a more purposeful daily routine.

From your knowledge of the Fair Access to Care Services bands, which band might Robert fall into? Write down an explanation of why Robert falls into the band you have chosen.

It is, of course, very difficult to make a judgment of this sort on the limited information that you have been given in the case study. It would be normal to make this decision after the gathering of comprehensive information through the development of a single assessment with a range of professionals. However, this activity enables you to think about the criteria and the complexity of applying them to specific situations with older adults. We would suggest that it is unlikely that Robert falls into the *critical* band, although in terms of *work*, *education or learning* and *social roles and responsibilities* you may have thought that the *substantial* band was appropriate. However, we would argue that the next band of *moderate* or even perhaps the *low* band may be the most appropriate, given the information we have. You will see, though, that the criteria within the bands is often only separated by subjective terms, such as *many aspects* as opposed to *several aspects* and *the majority* as opposed to *several*.

Partnership and participation

Near the start of this chapter, when you were learning about the general legal and political context of social work with older people, we introduced the concept of *citizenship* and the strength of the political voice that older people have, as they have influenced service developments at different levels across the country. Indeed, politically, older people have considerable influence in terms of voting power, sometimes referred to as *grey power*. Research by MORI has shown that people over 55 years of age have over four times the voting power of younger people, as there are twice as many older people and they are considered to be twice as likely to vote (MORI, 2001). In this section you will firstly look at how older people have participated in and been able to influence the development of social care services, through the specific examples of Better Government for Older People and the activi-

\ge Concern. The second part of this section will then introduce further examples of
 d legislation that focus on partnerships across health and social care agencies.

Better Government for Older People

Older people are among the biggest users of public services. But they often suffer from a failure to respond to their needs and listen to their voices. The Better Government for Older People pilots are at the forefront in finding innovative ways to make sure older people get the services they deserve. They are prime examples of how modernising government should work. (Rt Hon. Ian McCartney MP, Minister of State at the Cabinet Office, cited in BGOP, 1999)

The 'Better Government for Older People' initiative (BGOP) is a national programme that involves older people in influencing how services (not just social care, but all services that affect their lives) should be developed and shaped. It was established by the Cabinet Office in 1998 as a two-year programme that aimed to encourage local agencies to work together with older people to achieve active participation and citizenship. Initially 28 pilot projects were led by local authorities across the United Kingdom; at the same time a national Older People's Advisory Group (OPAG), drawn from the pilots, provided opportunities for the government to engage with older people. The OPAG continues to be one of the national lobbying groups for older people, influencing national and local policy and service provision.

Age Concern

Age Concern is an example of a national organisation that encourages and assists older people to participate in service developments locally and nationally. There are many other such organisations, but we have chosen to examine the work of Age Concern to illustrate the endeavours of a national group lobbying in the interests of older people. Through its campaigns, Age Concern raises public awareness of issues that affect older people and works with organisations to improve and develop services. The organisation prepares briefings for House of Commons and/or House of Lords debates, and also gathers together consultation and policy papers and brings them to the attention of older people. In this way, Age Concern, in consultation with older people in the regions and through their website, analyse current and proposed legislation to safeguard and preserve the rights and interests of older people. Through its information and advice services, Age Concern offers older people a comprehensive guide to the issues that may affect them. This includes not only social care issues, but also other concerns such as pensions, transport and housing.

So far, in this section, we have concentrated on partnerships with older adults and their carers. However, as you have seen from earlier discussions in this chapter, the modernisation agenda also reinforces the partnership between health and social care agencies (Means et al., 2003). The examples given below aim to provide you with an introduction to some of the more recent key documents that impact upon social work practice across professional boundaries in an inter-professional context. Further and more detailed discussion of partnership and participation in practice is also provided in Chapter 7 of this book.

The Health Act 1999

The Health Act 1999 provided agencies and social workers with an early indication of government proposals for the future development of partnership working across health and social care agencies. The NHS Plan, discussed below, was to consolidate and confirm the political priorities and vision in this respect. The Health Act created a *duty* of co-operation between NHS bodies and local authorities. The Act discounted the option of major organisational or structural change to achieve its aims; instead it provided the *power* for authorities to undertake some of the processes that would enable this, including joint arrangements for purchasing and providing services being made possible by changes in permissible funding and administrative arrangements. These became known as the Health Act *flexibilities*. Additionally, the Health Act 1999 introduced changes to primary health care structures and set up Primary Care Trusts to replace general practitioner fund-holding practices.

The National Health Service Plan 2000

The NHS Plan: A plan for investment, a plan for reform (DoH, 2000d) laid out the government's longer-term strategy for the National Health Service. While there is only one chapter that is specifically dedicated to 'Changes between health and social services', the whole document contains initiatives that impact upon developments in both health and social care. The main proposals are:

- greater emphasis on bringing health and social care services into the same buildings, for example GP surgeries;

- the development of new structures, Care Trusts, to commission and deliver health and social care;

- an increase in uptake of the financial 'flexibilities' introduced by the Health Act 1999 to enable integrated services to access joint budgets;

- the introduction of the NSF for Older People including investment in intermediate care services and the requirement for the single assessment process;

- the introduction of Care Direct, a new information and advice service covering health, social care and other related services.

(Glasby and Littlechild, 2004)

Health and Social Care Act 2001

This piece of primary legislation was intended to deliver many key aspects of the NHS Plan detailed above. The Act is separated into five parts:

- *Part 1* – makes changes to the structure and funding of the NHS and allows for the extension of public private partnerships in the NHS.

- *Part 2* – addresses pharmaceutical services.

- *Part 3* – creates new powers for the creation of Care Trusts by developing health and local authority local partnerships, including transfer of staff if necessary, to provide integrated care.

- *Part 4* – makes changes to the way that long-term care is funded and provided. This is particularly pertinent to care services for older people as section 49 of this Act separates nursing care from community care services and introduces *free nursing care*. This means that the NHS has to assess and pay for the costs of the registered nursing time where this is an element of the individual's care.

- *Part 5* – deals with patient information and stipulates when this information may be shared. It also looks at prescribing responsibilities in the NHS.

NHS Continuing Care Services – Guidance and circulars

The financing of long-term care, known as continuing health care, has been the source of much debate and contest both at a national level and across local agencies. Health and social care agencies will, understandably, want to clarify their respective responsibilities as the effect upon their budgets could be considerable. Additionally, health services care is provided free of charge to the service user, while social care services are most commonly charged for. The distinction becomes particularly sensitive where permanent care within an establishment is being considered, as the financial contribution required from the service user may accumulate significantly.

In 1995 the Department of Health issued detailed guidance to authorities on *NHS responsibilities for meeting continuing health care needs* (House of Commons Health Committee 1995). This guidance covered not only the types of service that would be within the NHS remit, but also dealt with the hospital discharge process and a procedure for review or complaint in respect of continuing care decisions. A later circular *Continuing Care: NHS and Local Councils' Responsibilities* (DoH, 2001b) was issued in 2001. This circular aims to update the guidance, following a number of ombudsman complaints and legal judgments, reinforcing the need for authorities to work together and to revise their review and complaints procedures for continuing care arrangements. You will find it interesting to examine your local health agency's continuing care policy, as often these policies and procedures are criticised for being restrictive and complex (Glasby and Littlechild, 2004: 46). More recently further circulars and ombudsman's decisions have led to more developments in *continuing care criteria*. For the latest situation and guidance you should visit the Department of Health website at **www.doh.gov.uk**.

Health and Social Care Act 2003

The Act formally set up the Commission for Social Care Inspection (CSCI) that has been described earlier in the chapter. It also establishes the Commission for Healthcare Audit and Inspection. It can be seen, therefore, that this statute further supports the government's modernisation agenda principles in that it makes provision for bodies that focus on accountability, quality, standards and inspection services.

Community Care (Delayed Discharges etc.) Act 2003

This Act of Parliament was implemented in January 2004, following the first mention of such a system within the NHS Plan 2002 (DoH, 2002d). It contains a controversial scheme whereby local authorities are charged for hospital beds that are unnecessarily taken up by people waiting for a social service. The term used for this charge, within the explanatory notes to the Act, is *reimbursement*. The regulations set out a daily amount that the local authority must *reimburse* to the relevant National Health Service agency where a person's discharge has been delayed due to a failure on the part of the local social services authority.

The regulations and directions to the Act set out, in considerable detail, the processes and procedures that must be followed by the relevant authorities. These documents also make the links to continuing care arrangements as discussed earlier in the chapter. The government intends that this legislation will lead to an expansion in domiciliary services while reducing the numbers of delayed discharges from acute hospital beds. It has only been possible to give a brief overview of the arrangements for delayed discharges; however, given the government's drive to develop partnership working, you should be able to discern potential contradictions in the requirements in this law. We would suggest that this process of one agency charging another for delays in arranging care could be seen to undermine joint working and lead to antagonism between the two agencies. Glasby and Littlechild (2004: 57) cite the House of Commons Health Committee, which suggested that the Act could lead to 'an unproductive culture of buck passing and mutual blame'. On the other hand, it is possible that such processes could result in strengthening the partnership as the two agencies may be determined to work together to avoid reimbursements in recognition that such monies would be more wisely spent in jointly developing appropriate services. This legislation also has the potential to impact adversely on older people, for if there is financial pressure to discharge them from a hospital bed, this may encourage discharge into inappropriate services. However, the government intends that the opposite will happen and that, in order to speed up discharges, local agencies will develop a greater range of appropriate and flexible services to meet assessed needs.

The foregoing sections have shown some examples of key documents that are relevant to contemporary social work practice with older adults in an inter-professional context. You will have noted that documents and legislation discussed in earlier sections of the chapter are also relevant to partnership approaches, such as the National Service Framework for Older People and the Care Standards Act 2000.

As you will appreciate, there is a plethora of policy, guidance and legislation that drives the priority of partnership, inter-agency and inter-professional collaboration. However, Means et al. (2003: 214) point out that despite this abundance of national directives and guidance, 'there has been little by way of incremental progress in joined-up working'. It is apparent that the boundary between what is considered to be health care and now defined as social care is shifting (Glasby and Littlechild, 2004: 58), but there is less confidence that consistent, effective joint working, across the boundaries, is being achieved in practice.

ACTIVITY 3.5

Sarah and Robert have agreed to receive a range of health and social care services. They have one detailed care plan that explains how these services will assist Robert with his mobility, particularly working with him to increase opportunities for social and recreational occupation. Robert has agreed to attend a local centre during the day, where a further, more detailed plan of activities will be drawn up. He has also been introduced to a volunteer, Clive, who works for a local charitable group and calls in to see Robert and play chess about once a week. Additionally, Robert continues to have regular appointments with his general practitioner, a visiting district nurse and at the hospital to monitor his health. Sarah enjoys the opportunity to go out when her husband is at the centre. She has also started to attend a carers' support group and has developed new, supportive friendships through this network.

From the continuation of the case study given above, write down your responses to the questions below;

- *What type of agencies could be involved in supporting this couple?*

- *What difference does the provider of services make?*

- *How could Robert and Sarah influence services?*

Although the case study information does not give you details of all the agencies that may be working to support Robert and Sarah, it is likely that the statutory sector is represented by health and social services provision. However, it is possible that the social care services, particularly the day and domiciliary support, while being purchased by the statutory social services, may be provided by a private organisation. Furthermore, the local area may have developed a Care Trust through which all of these statutory services are arranged. The voluntary sector is also providing a valuable service to support Robert and his carer. You may have thought that there are no discernable differences between the different providers and, indeed, often service users are unclear about which agency provides which element of their care package. Effective partnership working should result in the service being delivered by the most appropriate person and agency, with no need for divisions or boundaries to be apparent. However, one caveat exists within this ideal in that, as mentioned earlier, services provided by health agencies are not charged for at the point of delivery, whereas social care services most usually require a financial contribution to be paid by the service user.

Robert and Sarah could influence these services in many ways. They may directly work with the staff to explain their wishes and preferences; they will also have had an opportunity to shape the care plan. Their influence on the care plan will be reinforced and revisited each time the care plan is reviewed, as they will participate in the multi-agency, inter-professional review meetings. At another level, Robert and Sarah may decide to join relevant local or national organisations that lobby for appropriate care services for older people.

C H A P T E R   S U M M A R Y

In this chapter you have learnt about some examples of key areas of legislation, guidance and standards and their significance for social work practice with older people. It has not been possible to look at every piece of relevant legislation, guidance and policy, but through the use of specific examples and a consideration of their impact on practice, you will have increased your knowledge and understanding of social work practice with older people. This overview of the legal and political context of social work practice with older people will also support your reading of other chapters in this book, where particular legislation or policy initiatives may be examined in more depth.

In this chapter you have had the opportunity to increase your understanding of the main types of laws and some of the most commonly met terminology in this context. The main body of the chapter reflected the themes of the government's modernisation agenda and examined some of the most influential documents that support the implementation of those political priorities. Using the developing case study of Robert and Sarah, you will have been able to consider how these modernisation principles make a difference within social work practice situations with older adults.

It is important that you remain mindful that, although for the purposes of coherence in this text it has been necessary to look at each piece of legislation or guidance separately, in social work practice these requirements operate in a complex interrelated way that impacts upon all aspects of the organisation and practice of social work.

FURTHER READING

Mandelstram, M. (1999) *Community Care Practice and the Law*, 2nd edn. London: Jessica Kingsley.

Johns, R. (2003) *Using the Law in Social Work*. Exeter: Learning Matters.

WEBSITES

www.bgop.org.uk – Better Government for Older People (BGOP)
This site provides up-to-date news about the organisation's activities and enables access to various relevant publications and briefings.

www.legislation.hmso.gov.uk/acts
This is the Stationery Office (HMSO) site that provides access to all the legislation of the United Kingdom, along with explanatory notes and statutory instruments.

www.careandhealth.co.uk
This site is regularly updated with new and emerging policy and legislation. It has a specific section entitled 'policy watch' for this purpose and also provides links to the relevant Acts.

Chapter 4

Specific areas of social work practice with older people – mental health and learning disability

The subject skills highlighted to demonstrate this knowledge in practice include:

3.1.5 The nature of social work practice
- The nature and characteristics of skills associated with effective practice, both direct and indirect, with a range of service users and in a variety of settings including group care

3.2.2 Problem-solving skills
3.2.2.2 Gathering information
3.2.2.3 Analysis and synthesis
3.2.2.4 Intervention and evaluation
5.2.1 Knowledge and understanding
- Ability to use this knowledge and understanding in work within specific practice contexts

Introduction

The social work subject benchmark 3.1.1 describes the knowledge, understanding and skills required when working with service users. *The nature and validity of different definitions of, and explanations for, the characteristics and circumstances of service users* (in this case, older people) *and the services required by them* will be the focus of this chapter and the following chapter. In this chapter you will explore definitions, theoretical explanations, characteristics and related social work practice with older people who experience mental ill health and/or learning disability. The chapter will consider how these needs are defined and how the social work processes of assessment, planning, intervention and review can take account of the specific experiences and needs of older people. Throughout each section of the chapter you will be encouraged to consider the links to social work practice.

It is very important that you note and understand at this stage in your reading that mental ill health and learning disability are very different. Mental ill health can occur in episodes, with changes in the severity of the signs, whereas a learning disability is usually a permanent impairment of intellectual functioning that remains relatively constant. Furthermore, people can fully recover their health after having an episode of mental ill health as, unlike learning disabilities, mental ill health is not thought to originate from damage to the brain. Therefore this chapter is written in four parts. In the first part, you will explore the specific practice context of mental health in older adults; similarly in the second part of the chapter you will examine the context of social work practice with older adults who have learning disabilities. As you move into the third section of the chapter you will draw together your learning from the first two parts to consider the specific social work skills, methods and services that are associated with effective practice with older people whose lives are affected by mental ill health or learning disability. The final section of the chapter will give you the opportunity to review and summarise your learning from throughout the chapter, as you will draw together the themes and common issues from the first three parts of the chapter to look at the impact on older people's lives where they experience both mental ill health and learning disability.

Older people and mental health

It is not possible within this chapter to cover every possible form of mental ill health that older people may experience. For this reason, we have chosen to focus on older people's experience of depression and dementia as these conditions also form the focus of the National Service Framework for Older People (NSF), Standard 7 (DoH, 2001a). It is possible to debate whether dementia should be categorised as a mental or physical ill health, but the reality is that dementia impacts upon both mental and physical health. If you wish to extend your studies in respect of mental health further, we recommend Golightley (2004) who discusses severe mental ill health including psychotic illnesses in detail.

Terminology

In order to develop your understanding of social work practice with older people who have dementia or depression, you will need to understand how these notions are defined and explained. You will start by considering the prevalence of dementia before examining how this term and other frequently used, related words are defined. You will then focus on depression in older people in the same way.

Dementia

According to figures produced by the Alzheimer's Society, the number of people with dementia is steadily increasing, with the incidence rising with increasing age.

RESEARCH SUMMARY

Prevalence and incidence of dementia in the United Kingdom:

- *Using population figures for 2001, the number of people with dementia in England is over 650,000.*

- *Dementia affects one person in 20 aged over 65 years and one person in five over 80 years of age.*

The well-established prevalence rates for dementia in the UK are:

Age (years)	Prevalence
40–65	1 in 1,000
65–70	1 in 50
70–80	1 in 20
80+	1 in 5

Source: ***www.alzheimers.org.uk***

When considering what these figures mean in terms of social work practice and services for older people, you should firstly think about what we mean by 'dementia'.

The words and phrases that we use to describe our ideas have meanings and constructions attached to them. Some of these meanings, or common understandings, may be very apparent and deliberate, others may be less readily obvious, but can nonetheless indicate the attitudes and beliefs related to that term. For example, there are many different words that are used in everyday speech to refer to older people who have differing degrees of memory problems.

ACTIVITY 4.1

- *Make a list of all the words or phrases that you have used or heard used to describe older people with memory-related problems.*

- *Examine your list. What do these terms actually mean? Are there hidden assumptions or meanings within the words?*

You may have thought of words like *confused* or *senile*. *Confused* actually describes an experience that we will all go through at different times in our lives, whereas *senile* is a more complex word. The Internet dictionary site **www.dictionary.com** tells us that when the word *senile* was first recorded it had the neutral meaning of *pertaining to old age* but that, despite research demonstrating that memory and cognitive disorders are not a normal part of the ageing process, the term has taken on a negative connotation linked to mental decline.

If you have experience of working in health and social care settings, you may also have come across the acronyms EMI and ESMI. These are abbreviations of elderly mentally impaired (or ill) and elderly severely mentally impaired (or ill). We also thought of the following phrases: *person with an age-related memory problem or difficulty*; *person with a mental health problem*; *person with Alzheimer's disease*; and *person who has had a multi-infarct dementia*. We believe that the most important element of the term you choose is that you remember that people are individuals and that they are people first. In other words, if you choose to refer to 'the elderly' or 'the confused', you are effectively grouping people into one homogenous group and ignoring them as individual people.

In this book we are using the term 'dementia' which is defined within the NSF for Older People (DoH, 2001a: 96) as 'a clinical syndrome characterised by a widespread loss of mental function'. Dementia is most usually used to describe certain signs and characteristics that are commonly associated with memory loss in older adults. The Alzheimer's Society, which undertakes to research and disseminate information about dementia care, lists the following symptoms of dementia:

- Loss of memory – for example, forgetting the way home from the shops, or being unable to remember names and places.

- Mood changes – particularly as parts of the brain that control emotion are affected by disease. People with dementia may also feel sad, frightened or angry about what is happening to them.

- Communication problems – a decline in the ability to talk, read and write.

In the later stages of dementia, the person affected will have problems carrying out everyday tasks and will become increasingly dependent on other people.

(*Source*: **www.alzheimers.org.uk**)

The NSF for Older People lists six features of dementia:

- Memory loss

- Language impairment (having difficulty finding words especially names and nouns)

- Disorientation (not knowing the time or place)

- Change in personality (becoming more irritable, anxious or withdrawn; loss of skills and impaired judgment)

- Self neglect

- Behaviour which is out of character (for example, sexual disinhibition or aggression)
(DoH, 2001a: 96)

There may be a range of explanations for these experiences: physiological changes in the brain caused, for example, by a stroke or Alzheimer's disease; physiological changes elsewhere in the body, such as infection; or social and psychological changes. It is important to note that although the symptoms associated with dementia are likely to get gradually worse, this progression is dependent upon many factors and is by no means predictable. First, each older person is unique and their physiological, psychological, emotional, social and cultural lives will have a bearing on how they experience dementia. Additionally, predisposing or causative factors and the care subsequently provided may influence the severity and advancement of the symptoms.

You may come across different physiological diseases and conditions that can result in the features described above. Some examples are listed below:

- Alzheimer's disease;

- Creutzfeldt-Jakob disease (CJD);

- Pick's disease;

- dementia with Lewy bodies;

- vascular dementia.

As you can see, a number of these examples are framed with a medical label using the term 'disease'. Later in this chapter you will consider the debate between the physiological and the social approaches to explaining the symptoms that have been described here.

Depression
Evaluating the incidence and prevalence of depression among older people is not straightforward. Depression in this age group is often not identified (Age Concern, 2004; DoH, 2001a) and those studies that have been made have reached a number of different conclusions (SCIE, 2004).

RESEARCH SUMMARY

Prevalence and incidence of depression among older people

*A systematic review of community-based studies of adults aged 55 and over suggested that depression was comparatively common in later life (about 13.5%) but that the most severe forms of depression were relatively rare (1.8%). (Source: **www.scie.org.uk**)*

Depression in people aged 65 and over is especially under-diagnosed. At any one time, around 10–15% of the population aged 65 and over will have depression. More severe states of depression are less common, affecting about 3–5% of older people. (DoH, 2001a: 90–3)

It appears, therefore, that our understanding of the numbers of older people whose lives are being affected by depression is limited. The inconsistencies in our knowledge base in this respect should influence our work with older people, not only in terms of promoting good mental health and preventative approaches, but also ensuring early recognition of people's care needs through inter-professional working and holistic assessment practices. In order to develop your practice in this way, you need to ensure that you understand the meanings of the term 'depression' and other words that may be associated with it.

As you have seen in the section above, the words and phrases that we use can convey underlying assumptions or beliefs and are not always accurately descriptive of what we are trying to express.

ACTIVITY 4.2

In the same way as in Activity 4.1 where you looked at common words or phrases for older people who experience memory difficulties, in this activity you should think about the words you associate with depression.

- *Make a list of all the words or phrases that come to your mind when you think about the term depression.*

- *Examine your list. What do these terms actually mean? Are there hidden assumptions or meanings within the words?*

It is likely that you associate certain emotions with depression, such as sadness or hopelessness, or feeling lonely, withdrawn, even suicidal. These words are actually all some of the signs and symptoms that older people may experience if they become depressed. As with dementia, both the NSF for Older People (DoH, 2001a) and the Alzheimer's Society offer helpful definitions and lists of the more common characteristics.

The NSF for Older People states that:

Depression is a disorder of mood and may be characterised by:

- Low mood and feelings of sadness

- Loss of enjoyment

- Poor memory and concentration

- Tiredness and fatigue

- Unexplained pain

- Feelings of guilt

- Suicidal thoughts or impulses

- Delusions

(DoH, 2001a: 93–4)

The Alzheimer's Society explores depression and makes the links to the symptoms of dementia described above. According to the Alzheimer's Society:

Depression is a more persistent condition in which a number of feelings, such as sadness, hopelessness or lack of energy, dominate a person's life and make it difficult for them to cope.

(*Source*: **www.alzheimers.org.uk**)

Some of the common symptoms listed by the Society include:

A sad, hopeless or irritable mood for much of the time

Increased anxiety

Feelings of low self-esteem, worthlessness or undue guilt

Feelings of isolation and of being cut off from other people

Sleep disturbance, such as early waking

Problems with remembering, concentrating or making simple decisions

Slowing down in mind and body, or increased agitation and restlessness

Eating too little or too much, and weight loss or gain

Aches and pains that appear to have no physical cause

Thoughts of death and suicide

(Source: **www.alzheimers.org.uk**)

As with dementia the extent to which an individual who has depression experiences these symptoms will be different for each person. The causative factors are also likely to be complex and varied, again being influenced, for example, by the person's life course development, their immediate environment and any contributory factors such as a bereavement or sudden unwanted life change. In the next part of the chapter you will develop your understanding of some of the most influential explanations for dementia and depression in later adulthood.

Theoretical perspectives

In this chapter and in Chapter 5, you are developing your knowledge and understanding of work with older people within specific practice contexts. In order to develop a holistic approach to your practice, you need to become aware of the nature and validity of different explanations for the characteristics and circumstances of older people. In these two chapters, you will achieve this by examining the issues, for example in this section *dementia* and *depression* as experienced by older people, from two very different viewpoints: from a physiological or biological perspective and from a social perspective.

ACTIVITY 4.3

Read the short case study given below. As you read the experiences and events in the case study, note down how these might be explained. In other words, what might be the causative factors that lie beneath these occurrences?

Michael Watson is 73 years old and has lived all of his life in a rural town called Westfield. He has been married for the past 52 years, but his wife Sonia died suddenly while sleeping in the double bed next to Michael, recently. Michael and Sonia have no children. Prior to Sonia's death, Michael had been aware that he was forgetful at times. For example, he would walk into a room in the house, but then not remember why he was there. However, in the weeks following Sonia's death, Michael began to feel very confused. At times he experienced this as feelings of disorientation and his awareness of the situation made him very anxious, but also frustrated and angry with himself. Michael was not fully aware that his behaviours were causing concern to his neighbours and friends. Six weeks after Sonia's death, the police received a report from people living in a remote farmhouse some 12 miles out of Westfield. Michael had been found sitting motionless by a tree, dressed only in a pair of shorts. It was thought that he might have been there for more than 24 hours. Michael was very cold, emaciated, dehydrated and was not communicating. The outcome of police enquiries and health and social care assessment resulted in an emergency admission to residential care for further assessment of Michael's health and social care needs. In the care home it was quickly noted that Michael's behaviours were unpredictable. At times he was aggressive both verbally and physically, at other times he was quiet, withdrawn and tearful. Michael hardly slept at night, preferring to wander around the home, often disturbing other residents. He also often refused food and was found urinating in the corners of rooms in the home.

There are many possible explanations for Michael's behaviours and experiences, some of these may depend upon the perspective, or the theoretical approach, that you have taken. Here we are going to examine two particular models, the medical model of disability and the social model of disability, and comment on Michael's situation from both perspectives. Figure 4.1 outlines some examples of how an older person's needs might be interpreted from these two approaches. You may find it helpful to refer back to this diagram and your notes on the case study as you work through the information below about the two models.

THE MEDICAL MODEL

THE SOCIAL MODEL

Society puts up a range
of barriers that are
disabling this
older person

There is something
wrong with this person

This person needs
treatment or a cure

In this society the
environment and
transportation are
inaccessible

This person needs care

In this society, attitudes
and values towards older
people are discriminatory
and judgmental

This person needs special
equipment or services

In this society there is
a lack of employment
opportunities, low
incomes and poverty

This person cannot do
what everyone else can do

Society excludes and
segregates some people,
treating them as though
they were different, e.g.
older people, disabled
people

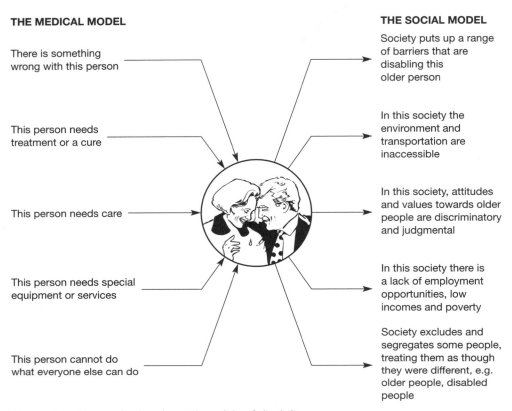

Figure 4.1 *The medical and social models of disability*

The medical model of disability

A physiological or biological approach to explaining disability starts from the perspective that the circumstances of someone's life result directly or entirely from illness, disease, bodily changes and physical, biological or sensory impairments. Parker and Bradley (2003:76) describe the medical model as one that *focuses on physical deficits and on individual health needs*. Attention to these factors in an assessment of the case study situation above could lead to an assumption that Michael has a dementia-type disease or depression. Furthermore, the perspective taken, in this case the physiological or biological perspective, informs the intervention that follows. In other words, using a medical model in this way could result in medication or medical treatments that aim to cure the behaviours.

The physiological or medical model has been strongly criticised for being reductionist (Kitwood, 2002:229). This means that it brings the explanation down to bodily changes or disease and nothing more, omitting to consider any other influences on the person's circumstance and focusing solely on the individual. As you can see in Figure 4.1, the arrows from the medical model are pointing towards the person and the explanations suggest the individual is responsible for their situation. Such a narrow explanation could result in false assumptions or judgments about people. For example, the common notion that it is impossible to communicate with people who have dementia creates a seriously disabling barrier in the lives of older people with dementia (Morris, 1997). Pritchard (2001:74), in her description of interviews with older men who had experienced abusive situations, describes how slight confusion can result from such abuse and yet 'entries had been made on their files that they were suffering with "severe dementia" which was definitely not true in either case'. Some of the most convincing challenges to the medical model are made by Kitwood (1993, 2002) whose arguments are summarised in the Research summary below.

RESEARCH SUMMARY

Depersonalisation

Kitwood argues that care provision 'contains the residues of at least four depersonalising traditions: bestialisation, the attribution of moral deficit, warehousing and the unnecessary use of a medical model' (2002: 230).

Malignant social psychology

Kitwood uses this term to describe his observations of care settings. He explains that:

> *The strong word 'malignant' signifies something very harmful, symptomatic of a care environment that is deeply damaging to personhood, possibly even undermining physical well-being.... The malignancy is part of our cultural inheritance. (2002: 230).*

Kitwood argues that using a medical or 'technical frame' is to take an approach like a mechanic working on a car or machine, thus denying the importance of the individual, the person and 'personhood'. Kitwood also tells us that the technical frame has long been the dominant frame in working with older people who have dementia (1993: 100).

Social work with older people from this perspective would prioritise, respect and focus on a wider view of the individual and their situation, including psychological and sociological perspectives (Kitwood, 1990). Bearing in mind the approach proposed by Kitwood, the next section considers what is meant by the social model of disability and how this could be seen to be directly in opposition to the physiological, medical model.

The social model of disability

The social model of disability has been written about extensively since the late 1980s when movements of disabled people began to campaign and challenge widely accepted views of disability. The key difference between this perspective and the medical model set out above is that this viewpoint considers the social oppression that is experienced by people with a disability and places the problem within society, whereas the medical model locates the disability with the person (Oliver, 1996). In Figure 4.1 above, you can see how for the social model of disability the arrows are all pointing away from the person and the explanations suggest that society is responsible for the individual's situation. This model identifies the barriers to full inclusion in society that are experienced by people with impairments. Although the approach originated from the views of physically disabled people, the perspective has grown to be widely accepted as relevant to all forms of impairment in all age groups. The social model of disability is strongly identified with service user empowerment, enabling services to focus on the desired outcomes of users

(Statham, 2004). Statham (2004:15) also informs us that the social model is strongly linked to *holistic* and *ecological* approaches to practice, both of which are terms that are preferred by some black and minority ethnic groups. However, there have been some well-formed arguments that criticise some aspects of the social model. For example, Vernon (2002) raises concern that multi-oppressions resulting from gender, sexual orientation and race are not addressed when using this model.

If you return to your notes on the case study, you may find that many of the ways in which you thought that Michael's experiences could be explained could be seen to originate from a sociological perspective, in other words through a social model that also acknowledges the interplay between social and interpersonal factors. For example, Michael may be refusing to eat in the care home because he does not like the food or it does not meet with his cultural or religious dietary needs. He may be urinating in inappropriate places because he is a little disorientated by the sudden change in his environment and has not been given adequate support and guidance to find his way around. Michael's recent bereavement must have a profound affect upon how he thinks and behaves at this time. It is likely that his self-esteem has been lowered as he may blame himself for sleeping as Sonia died. He also has to reappraise his identity and his pattern of life as a widower without the support of his long-term partner. Essentially, we could make a great number of assumptions about Michael's situation and how he feels, but only Michael could really begin to tell us and it is likely to be extremely sensitive and difficult for him to do so at this time.

We have shown how these two approaches to understanding and explaining people's circumstances can be seen to be in direct conflict. However, we would not wish to discard either approach but would recommend a holistic approach to social work practice whereby all perspectives are incorporated and understood, particularly and most importantly the views of the individual and the meaning they attach to their circumstances. In this way the older person's psychological, sociological and biological needs will be addressed within the context of their individual lives.

In this first part of the chapter you have looked at two examples of mental ill health that affect the lives of some older people in our society: dementia and depression. You have considered the prevalence of such disorders among older people and have learnt about some of the words and phrases that are used to describe the disorders and associated signs. Finally you have read about competing theoretical explanations related to these disorders. You will use your knowledge from this part of the chapter in later parts, where you will increase your understanding about the particular practice skills that you need to develop in order to practise effectively with older people experiencing mental ill health. First, though, you will consider the context of practice with older people who have learning disabilities.

Older people and learning disability

The government's strategy for learning disability for the twenty-first century, the White Paper *Valuing People* (DoH, 2001b), has arguably been the most influential document for services for people with learning disabilities for many years. However, there is little mention in the White Paper of the needs of older people with learning disabilities, except in one section towards the end of the document (pages 103–4) where effectively readers are directed to the NSF for Older People (DoH, 2001a). The *Valuing People* strategy's director of implementation has commented that 'the major improvements to people's lives secured under the Valuing People white paper must be extended to older people with learning difficulties' (Community Care, 2004).

Later in this part of the chapter you will learn more about national requirements and services for older people with learning disabilities. Firstly, though, you will need to consider what we mean by learning disability and whether there are many older people who fall into this category. The Research summary given below provides some statistical information about the numbers of people who are considered to have learning disabilities and their ages.

RESEARCH SUMMARY

How many people have learning disabilities?

Producing precise information on the number of people with learning disabilities in the population is difficult. In the case of people with severe and profound learning disabilities, we estimate there are about 210,000: around 65,000 children and young people, 120,000 adults of working age and 25,000 older people. In the case of people with mild/moderate learning disabilities, lower estimates suggest a prevalence rate of around 25 per 1000 population – some 1.2 million people in England [see Figure 4.2].

People with severe learning disabilities are those who need significant help with daily living. People with mild/moderate learning disabilities will usually be able to live independently with support.

(DoH, 2001b:15)

It can be seen, therefore, that there are significant numbers of older people who have mild/moderate learning disabilities and smaller numbers with severe learning disabilities. However, these figures are taken from 1999 and the White Paper also tells us that 'many people with learning disabilities now in their 50s and 60s were not expected to outlive their parents. Improved medical and social care now means they are living longer'. (DoH, 2001b:103). Thus, as time moves on, the demographic projections, using the graph shown in Figure 4.2, must be that there will be increasing numbers of older adults with learning disabilities. Additionally those adults are, in keeping with all adults in the population, likely to experience a range of physical, social, environmental and psychological changes associated with later life.

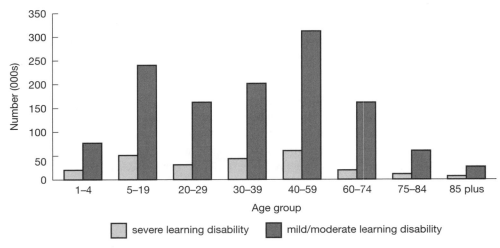

Figure 4.2 *People with learning disabilities, 1999*

Terminology

Earlier in this chapter and in other parts of this book, you have developed your appreciation of how words that are commonly used in our society and images that pervade our lives have socially constructed meanings that can lead to assumptions and prejudices which impact upon the lives of older people. As you have seen, in this book, we are using the term *learning disability*.

The *Valuing People* White Paper (DoH, 2001b) states that

Learning disability includes the presence of:

- a significantly reduced ability to understand new or complex information, to learn new skills (impaired intelligence), with;

- a reduced ability to cope independently (impaired social functioning);

- which started before adulthood, with a lasting effect on development.

(DoH, 2001b:14)

We have chosen to use the phrase older people with a learning disability to reflect the terminology used in the *Valuing People* White Paper (DoH, 2001b), as we find the definition helpful in that it takes a holistic perspective and encompasses intelligence, social functioning and development. However, these and other words used to describe the needs of the specific group of older people that we are considering in this part of the chapter are worthy of further exploration.

ACTIVITY 4.4

Look at the words and phrases listed below. Have you used or heard these terms used? Which of the terms do you feel are most appropriate and accurate in describing people who have learning disabilities? Try to rank them in order with number one being the most appropriate. Then write a brief explanation to support your reasoning for this choice. It would be useful if you could compare your notes with a colleague or fellow student and to think together about which of these terms older people who have learning disabilities might rank at number one for themselves.

- *Learning disabilities*

- *Mentally handicapped*

- *Learning difficulty*

- *Backward*

- *Special needs*

- *Learning impairment*

This Activity may seem straightforward, but it does not have one correct or incorrect answer. It is likely that you ranked learning disability as number one – indeed there is no doubt that at this time in the United Kingdom learning disability is the most commonly and officially used of the above terms (Race, 2002:4). Race (2002) explains that the social model of disability, described earlier in this chapter, views disability as the barriers that people with impairments encounter as a result of societal structures and attitudes. Consequently, according to Race (2002:4) the term learning disability taken literally means societal barriers to learning. In the same way, the social model of disability interprets learning impairment in a particular way. Impairment is given a biological meaning related to specific physical or psychological attributes. Therefore if the societal obstacles were eradicated or reduced, the disability that people experience as a result of their impairments would be correspondingly eradicated or reduced.

The term learning difficulty, according to Race (2002), would be the preferred words of service users, but this term is most often seen used within the context of educational policies and legislation which suggest that learning difficulty refers to a long-term condition that impacts upon the person's ability to learn. There are more detailed definitions on the government's disability website at **www.disability.gov.uk**. Similarly, you may have come across the words 'special needs' within an educational setting. This expression is also open to much debate: firstly, in terms of definition, it actually tells us very little. However, more importantly you should question whether we should consider certain groups of people to have special needs or whether society and the environment should be adjusted in such ways as to take account of all of its members' needs, so that those individuals who have impairments do not feel different or special. This, of course, reflects the viewpoint expressed through the social model of disability.

It is likely that when you completed Activity 4.4, you ranked the terms mentally handicapped and backward to the bottom of your list. You will recall from your reading of earlier parts of this chapter that it is important in our language to recognise and emphasise that we are talking about people as individuals, not merely labelling one homogeneous group suggesting all members of the group are the same. Therefore, the first problem with these terms is that they lack this recognition: they make no mention of the person. Additionally, these terms are very outdated, with mentally handicapped being widely accepted in the 1970s and 1980s as a classification for groups of people with certain behaviours. The term is also associated, by some people, with a notion of dependency and being cap-in-hand, with the additional complication that the use of the word 'mentally' within this phrase adds to common confusions between mental ill health and learning disabilities.

In our society we clearly need words and phrases that will help us to communicate and make sense of the world around us. However, some words and phrases, like those discussed above, serve as good examples of how meanings become attached to commonly used terms and subsequently lead to assumptions and prejudices which impact upon the lives of older people. In effect, we are attributing labels to human beings and because of the common understandings related to those labels, we make judgments. These stereotypical views and socially constructed identities then result in stigma and oppression. In the next section of the chapter you will look at the concept of normalisation, which is considered to be a process by which labelling and stigma can be countered.

Theoretical perspectives

In the first part of this chapter you looked at the nature and validity of two competing explanations of how older people experience dementia and depression: a physiological or biological perspective and a social perspective. The medical model and the social model are equally applicable when considering the lives of older people with learning disabilities. You could think about the different approaches that each of these models would take to explain the experience of having a learning disability in later life.

In this part of the chapter, you will learn about another perspective that, much like the social model of disability, presents a challenge to the medical model. You will develop your understanding of what is meant by 'normalisation' and 'social role valorisation' (SRV), both of which have been influential in the development of services for people with learning disabilities. However, in our view, these concepts are relevant in all areas of society, not only social care, and for all groups of disadvantaged people. Therefore we would argue that this approach can be developed in services for all older people, not only those who have learning disabilities.

In earlier parts of the chapter you have considered different terms or labels that describe groups of people. You have also considered how such labels can result in stigma and oppression of vulnerable groups in society. These notions of stigma, oppression and disadvantage underpin the development of normalisation as an approach that attempts to offset the negative influence of stigma. Wolfensberger and Tullman (2002:138) provide a succinct definition of normalisation as '...the use of culturally valued means in order to enable, establish, and/or maintain valued social roles for people'. You will see from the definition that there are clear links to social work values and back to your reading in Chapter 1 of this book.

> *...the foundation of normalisation, as of SRV, is an understanding, at both a conceptual and emotional level, of the power and effects of devaluation, on individuals, groups, and whole sections of society. (Race, 2002:193; original emphasis)*

The fundamental philosophy of normalisation and SRV is that we should challenge some of the social constructions and concepts that are accepted as normal in our society. This philosophy can also be seen to underpin the recent national strategies that you have previously explored and which are important to how services for older people and services for people with learning disabilities are developed and experienced.

> *Older people should no longer be seen as a burden on society. They are a vital resource of wisdom, experience and talent. (DoH, 2001a:2)*

> *Improving the lives of people with learning disabilities requires commitment nationally and locally to strong principles, a firm value base and clear objectives for services. Each individual should have the support and opportunity to be the person he or she wants to be. (DoH, 2001b:23)*

Race (2002:203) demonstrates how the *Valuing People* White Paper (DoH, 2001b) reflects the principles of SRV, in that all of the seven (out of the total eleven) objectives that relate to outcomes for people with learning disabilities can be seen in terms of providing valued roles.

The ideas that led to normalisation and SRV first emerged about fifty years ago and were related to the care that people received in long-stay institutions. The argument is that, by occupying valued, positive, social and economic roles, individuals will gain respect, dignity and confidence. One of the main criticisms of this approach is that simply by raising the need to value the role of vulnerable people in society you are, by implication, reinforcing the fact that their current status is devalued (Race, 2002) and in this way potentially perpetuating the oppression. However, you have seen how the fundamental values that underpin these approaches can be seen to be influencing contemporary social work services and practice. It is also evident that much of this influence has been brought about through the lobbying of older people and people with learning disabilities themselves, who want to raise awareness of their situation in society.

CASE STUDY

Margaret was brought up by her mother after her father died in the Second World War. Until two years ago, Margaret and her mother had lived in the same house in a small town. Then two years ago at the age of 88 years, Margaret's mother died. Despite Margaret having a moderate level of learning disability and her mother having had a number of physical difficulties, neither woman was known to social workers or social care services. As Margaret's mother grew older and her physical dependency had increased, so Margaret had attended to her mother's care needs. When her mother died, Margaret was 65 years old and had never been in paid employment and had only experienced social interactions with immediate family and neighbours.

Now, two years on, following work with a range of health and social care professionals, Margaret lives in a supported living environment where her independence is maximised. She also works part-time, in a supported environment, as a catering assistant in a large residential establishment for older people. Margaret is using the skills she developed when caring for her mother. She gets great satisfaction and enjoyment from the work as she enjoys interacting with the residents and meeting the many visitors to the home. The staff in the home greatly value her contribution to their service as they find her a diligent, willing and pleasant member of their team.

You have now worked through two parts of the chapter, the first which looked at issues of mental ill health and older people through the specific examples of dementia and depression, followed by this section in which you have considered the context of social work practice with older people who have learning disabilities. Having developed your knowledge in respect of these specific areas of social work practice, in the next part of the chapter you will learn about particularly relevant social work practice skills.

Social work practice with older people

Mental health services for older people should be able to respond effectively to individual needs, and take account of the social and cultural factors affecting recovery and support.

The hallmark of good mental health services is that they are: comprehensive, multidisciplinary, accessible, responsive, individualised, accountable and systematic.

(DoH, 2001a:91)

The NSF for Older People will set out a framework that applies to services for all people over 65 years of age. But for people with learning disabilities the ageing process may begin much earlier. This means that planning for the needs of 'older people' with learning disabilities may need to include a more extended population, perhaps taking account of those aged from 50 years upwards. Developing the person-centred approach to planning services ... will enable local agencies to address the needs of older people with learning disabilities. (DoH, 2001b:104)

The NSF for Older People and the *Valuing People* White Paper can be seen therefore to set the standard that services should respond effectively to individual need. In terms of social work practice, this is affected through the core social work processes of assessment, planning, intervention, monitoring and review. Both of these documents also stress the importance of a multi-disciplinary approach. This would be integral throughout these processes but is a particular feature of the single assessment process (SAP), which would be the form of assessment employed when working with older people. The SAP, as an example of partnership working, is discussed in more detail in Chapter 7 of this book.

In essence, when undertaking these processes with older people, whether they are experiencing mental ill health or have a learning disability, you will use the same skills as with any other assessment (SCIE, 2004). For the rest of this part of the chapter, you will concentrate on some of the skills that are important to social work practice with older people who have forms of dementia or depression or have learning disabilities. For further elaboration and detail on the social work processes, we recommend Parker and Bradley (2003).

Communication skills

The importance of effective communication skills when working with older people cannot be underestimated. As a social worker you will need to be able to both successfully convey and receive information between yourself and the older person you are working with. This process of two-way communication is central, not only to ensuring that the older person's needs and circumstances are fully understood, but also to the basis of empowerment through the provision of accessible, comprehensible information. You will need to give thought to how you recognise issues of language and culture. Most importantly you must ensure that the ways in which you communicate are sensitive to the needs of the older person, and that you are flexible and responsive as you work with them.

Communicating with older people who have types of dementia, for example, may be very challenging as they may encounter certain thoughts or beliefs that are unrealistic or seem unusual. Their understanding of your role, for example, may be distorted by other ideas and emotions that they are currently feeling. It is, therefore, all the more important that you find imaginative and responsive ways in which to engage the older person in dialogue to which they can meaningfully participate.

In services that have been developed for people with learning disabilities a range of innovative communication methods have been developed. However, as a social worker, you still need to ensure, as you work with each individual older person, that the skills and methods you choose are the most appropriate. Different ways of improving the communication between yourself and the service-user could include: using sign language; using pictorial representations; ensuring that you use very clear and plain language; enlisting the help of someone known well to the person, perhaps their keyworker or informal carer, who may have developed particular ways of communicating effectively with that person; using audio-visual materials. The content and subject matter of your interaction can also impact upon the effectiveness of how it is received and understood. Thus, no matter how straightforward you make the language, you are a professional with powers, certain roles and expectations to fulfil. However, communication is often facilitated through a personable, friendly approach, showing genuine interest in the individual and their lives. So, for example, giving attention to someone's life story, their history, family and their background, can often be a valuable starting point to earning their trust and respect.

Assessing and managing risk

The assessment and management of risk is a highly specialised area within which there has been a wealth of research, writing and developing models of practice. However, as you have been reading about social work practice with older people who have mental ill health or learning disabilities, it is important that safety and risk issues are raised. Parker and Bradley (2003:76) state that risk assessment is 'an important tool for practitioners to monitor and be alert to a range of consequences'; they cite the work of McDonald (1999) in defining the assessment of risk as 'a balancing process in which the application of judgement is brought to bear'. Indeed, the situation when working with older people who are deemed at risk to themselves or others because of certain behaviours related to mental ill health or learning disability is one that requires professional judgment. Most usually, that judgment should be made by the inter-professional team as a result of a full risk assessment, undertaken with the older person, as part of the single assessment process. Any such assessment should focus on the older person's strengths, their abilities, their views, wishes and feelings.

We all take numerous risks every day of our lives; these are usually the result of making our own assessment, or judgment, determining the balance ourselves between the benefits and the dangers that are apparent. We may not always do this consciously or knowingly and our decisions will often be influenced by previous experiences, again without us necessarily being aware of these thoughts. For users of social work services and for their carers, these judgments become part of a more formalised process involving a range of professionals. It is therefore very easy for the older person to become disempowered and not involved in making their own decisions about the risks involved.

The *balancing* process of risk assessment and risk management is often one where minimising one risk may result in raising another. The two case studies below are provided to give examples of how such situations can arise.

CASE STUDY

Gordon is 82 and has been diagnosed with Alzheimer's-type dementia. He has recently moved into a small residential care home. Gordon likes to go out and walk around the grounds of the care home and there were no perceived problems in him doing so until on three occasions he had become verbally aggressive to people passing by and other residents who were sitting out. The staff made a decision that Gordon should not be allowed out unaccompanied, and that due to staffing levels he would be accompanied at certain controlled times of the day. Almost as soon as these restrictions were imposed Gordon's behaviour worsened within the home and he became frequently verbally and physically violent.

Susan is 76 and has a learning disability. Susan has attended day care services for many years. Susan is known to have little understanding of how to manage her money, therefore, over the years, a system has been in place whereby she is given very small, set amounts of cash to buy sweets or personal things at the centre on each visit. Recently Susan's handbag was snatched when she was outside of the centre; her purse with the little bit of cash was inside. Susan was distraught. After the incident, the staff at the centre decided that Susan was too vulnerable to carry cash and that in the future she would not be given this money to carry but staff would go with her whenever she wanted to pur-chase anything. Susan did not understand why her money was not being given to her and took this as a punishment. Within a few weeks, she started to steal money from other day centre attendees so that she could buy the things she liked as she had always done.

The examples of Gordon and Susan's situations demonstrate some of the difficult judgments that have to be made when assessing risk. As you think about these case studies, it would be useful for you to link your ideas to the work of Kitwood (1990, 1993) discussed earlier in this chapter. Consider the emphasis he put on *personhood* and that professionals should empower older people rather than making the situation worse for them.

Services to meet the needs of older people

In the introduction to this part of the chapter you read about how the NSF for Older People (DoH, 2001a) highlights the need for 'comprehensive, multidisciplinary, accessible, responsive, individualised, accountable and systematic' services. These standards apply to all health and social care services for older people regardless of the setting.

Social care services to support older people with mental ill health or with a learning disability and their carers are provided in a range of different ways in different settings. These are sometimes specialist services, where all the service users will have been assessed as having similar needs, but they are sometimes integrated services where many different forms of care needs can be met. There are differing views on the appropriateness and suitability of different forms of service provision. The next Activity asks you to think about the strengths and weaknesses of these different approaches and to form your own views on the appropriateness of such services. After the Activity you will read about some of the arguments that have been put forward in this respect.

ACTIVITY **4.5**

Segregation or integration?

Using the knowledge you have gained from reading this chapter so far, think about the sort of care needs that older people with mental ill health or learning disabilities may have.

- *Make a list of all the different forms of social care service provision that could meet these needs (for example, residential care, day services and so on)*

- *In your opinion is it more appropriate to provide these services*

  (a) *as specialist services purposely developed to meet the needs of older people with mental ill health or older people who have learning disabilities; or*

  (b) *as integrated services that are purposely developed to meet a range of social care needs including those of older people who have mental ill health and/or learning disabilities?*

Write down a few bullet points to justify your choice. Why, in your opinion, are services most effectively configured in this way?

As we stated before the Activity, there are differing views on the issue of segregation or integration, but the issues are largely the same regardless of the type of service you are considering. You will have thought of many different types of service and the titles you use for them may differ according to where you live; we shall, therefore, not be defining the names of services in this chapter. The agency arranging and delivering the service will also vary according to where you live, with some services being multi-agency services. Some examples of types of social care service are: residential care; day care; respite care in an establishment; domiciliary care (home care); supported accommodation; sheltered accommodation; mobile warden service; community team outreach support; mobile meals; assistive technology in the home; advocacy; intermediate care service; adult placement schemes; step-down services; rapid response services – you may have thought of others.

As you thought about the second part of the activity your starting point may have been to consider which form of service you would prefer if you had care needs. You may also have thought about someone close to you, a friend or family member, and tried to imagine which type of service you would want for them. Some people would feel strongly that the services should reflect everyday society and be inclusive, in other words they should meet many types of needs and include a range of people. Others would argue that only specialist services can meet complex care needs and that where people who experience similar issues are together they can support and understand each other.

Hughes (1995:46) states that 'people seem to want to live in mixed communities and not segregated only with people with whom they might share one particular characteristic'. This argument could be seen to be supported by the reading you have done earlier, as you looked at *normalisation* and issues of *labelling*. However, others would argue that complex care needs require specially trained staff working in specialist care services. Furthermore, families and friends of people in residential or day care settings may feel it is inappropriate for the person they care about to be living or spending time in a setting where others have more complex needs.

RESEARCH SUMMARY

Integrated services for older people with learning disabilities

Hogg and Lambe (1998) have undertaken a review of the literature on residential services and family care-giving for older people with learning disabilities. In their working paper they cite a range of research that argues that 'where "valued" services for older people are available, integration into these is feasible and desirable'.

The major examples of such programmatic work have been described by Janicki (1993), Janicki and Keefe (1992) and LePore and Janicki (1990). Here successful integration of people with learning disabilities into generic services for elderly people, including residential provision, was demonstrated. Importantly, these publications deal in depth with the strategies for achieving successful integration and the barriers to successfully achieving such outcomes. (Hogg and Lambe, 1998: 31–2)

If there is to be a straight answer to the second part of the question we posed in Activity 4.5, then the first words of the quotation that we have provided above is, in our view, the clue. Rather than whether services are integrated or segregated, whether they are considered inclusive or exclusive, what is most significant is whether they are valued, high-quality services. It is our view that services should be led by the needs, wishes and feelings of the older people who need them and that this aspiration can only be achieved by providing, not only the vast range of service types that we have already seen, but providing those services in a variety of ways. Where both integrated and specialist quality services are available the older person has a genuine choice about how their needs are met.

In this part of the chapter you have developed your knowledge in respect of social work practice and services related to work with older people experiencing mental ill health or learning disability. As stated earlier, all of the skills and processes that are characteristic of good social work practice are relevant to work with older people and their carers, so in this part of the chapter we have only focused on some of the specific skills and services that are important to the practice context of social work with older people who have forms of dementia, depression or learning disabilities.

Older people with mental ill health and learning disabilities

This is the final part of Chapter 4, so you will be reviewing your learning and drawing together the themes from the first three parts of the chapter. You will do this by considering the impact on older people's lives where they experience both mental ill health and learning disability.

According to Mind (**www.mind.org.uk**), 'it is well known that people with learning disabilities are more vulnerable to mental health problems and psychiatric illnesses than the general population'. In their factsheet, Mind cite the work of Mansell (1993) in declaring that 'it is estimated that up to half of adults with learning disabilities also have additional mental health needs'. In order to explore these assertions further we have chosen to look in more depth at how older people with learning disabilities, particularly in this case Down's syndrome, may develop dementia and what this means for social work practice.

> *RESEARCH SUMMARY*
>
> ### Incidence and prevalence of dementia in adults with Down's syndrome
>
> *Holland et al. (1998) undertook a study to investigate the extent of clinical change with age in a sample of older people with Down's syndrome. The people in the sample were assessed for changes in memory, personality, general mental functioning and daily living skills. The study concluded that* 'the age-related pattern of presentation and dementia diagnoses differs from that seen in the general elderly population. However, age-specific prevalence rates of Alzheimer's disease were similar but 30–40 years earlier in life'. *(Holland et al., (1998).*

Down's syndrome and dementia

Through the Growing Older with Learning Disabilities programme at the Foundation for People with Learning Disabilities, Turk et al. (2001) reported the following facts in their Briefing for Commissioners:

At least 36% of people with Down's syndrome aged 50–60 years and 54.5% aged 60–69 are affected by dementia (compared to 5% of general population aged over 65 years). The prevalence increases significantly with age. *Turk et al., (2001)*

The research referred to above provides us with evidence that there are significant numbers of people who are likely to experience complex needs as they grow older as a result of having Down's syndrome and a dementia. Additionally, you must remember that these individuals may also experience the physical, emotional, social, environmental and psychological changes that are considered commonplace for all people as they age in our society.

In the detailed reports that accompany the research that we have summarised, complex biological explanations are offered for the changes that have been observed through investigation. However, earlier in this chapter you have developed your understanding of how a social model of disability and the concepts of normalisation or social role valorisation can help us to take a different perspective on older people's experiences. This is particularly relevant where an individual finds they have been attributed with two labels or diagnoses – learning disability and mental ill health – as the potential for stigma and oppression are likely to be significantly multiplied.

In terms of care provision to meet the needs of older people with complex needs, the debate between integrated and segregated services is again relevant. For if people are categorised into specific services because these services have the expertise to meet their particular needs, then a decision would have to be made as to whether learning disability services, older people's services or services specifically for older people with dementia would be most appropriate – unless, of course, a very specific service for those older people with learning disabilities and dementia was available. Working in this way tends only to further label people, as we would be effectively 'pigeon-holing' them into services. In the same way as we discussed earlier, the most appropriate way to meet an individual's care needs is thorough inter-professional assessment and quality, person-centred services that are chosen by the older person and that can demonstrate that they can meet those assessed needs.

Assessing and providing services for older adults who have learning disabilities and mental ill health requires robust co-ordination between all relevant agencies that should start with the single assessment process. Turk et al. (2001) state that by 30 years of age, people with Down's syndrome should have baseline assessments of cognitive and social functioning to assist future diagnosis and assessment. Baseline assessments would support proactive planning both at the strategic and at the individual level. The progressive nature of dementia is well known and the likely future needs of this group of people should inform service developments. Equally, at the individual level, as services are planned, professionals should consider the person's likely future needs so that minimal disruptions and changes to services are necessary as the person's needs change.

The social work involvement in assessment, care planning, monitoring and reviewing processes is a significant factor in developing a holistic approach. As a social worker you will have the opportunity to contribute a social perspective alongside empowering the older person and enabling them to influence the interventions and services. However, even though you will work in an inter-professional context, you must work within the agreed values and standards of social work practice, managing and being accountable for your own work. The two core mechanisms that will support you with this are supervision and support within your own organisation and using the skills of reflective practice. As you develop your skills of reflective practice and become self-critical and able to ask questions about the outcomes that your interventions have effected for older people, so you will find that you gain confidence and develop as a skilled social work professional.

C H A P T E R   S U M M A R Y

This chapter has focused on helping you to meet the social work subject benchmark 3.1.1 which requires you to understand 'the nature and validity of different definitions of, and explanations for, the characteristics and circumstances of service users [in this case, older people] and the services required by them.' You have achieved this by reading and working through activities that explore definitions, theoretical explanations, characteristics and related social work practice with older people who experience mental ill health and/or learning disabilities. The chapter started by looking separately at issues related to older people with mental ill health and issues related to older people with learning disabilities. In the last two sections of the chapter the issues were integrated to consider, firstly, specific social work practice relevant to older people whose lives are affected by mental ill health or learning disability and, secondly, the needs of older adults who experience both mental ill health and learning disability. In this way, the final parts of the chapter have provided an opportunity to review and reflect upon your learning.

FURTHER READING

Golightley, M. (2004) *Social Work and Mental Health*. Exeter: Learning Matters.

Race, D. (ed.) (2002) *Learning Disability – A Social Approach*. London: Routledge.

While neither of these texts are specific to the needs of older people, both offer an opportunity to explore these particular areas of social work practice in further depth. Both Golightley (2004) and Race (2002) take a social perspective on their analysis of policy, service and practice issues in their subject area.

WEBSITES

www.alzheimers.org.uk – The Alzheimer's Society
This is a very informative website that provides access to a range of factsheets, information about relevant research and useful guidance on caring for, and working with, people who experience dementia and/or related depression.

www.learningdisabilities.org.uk – The Foundation for People with Learning Disabilities
This is a comprehensive and easily navigated website run by a UK charity that researches issues related to learning disabilities.

Chapter 5

Specific areas of social work practice with older people – sensory impairment and physical impairment

This chapter will help you to begin to meet the following National Occupational Standards:

Key Role 1: Prepare for and work with individuals, families, carers, groups and communities to assess their needs and circumstances

- Prepare for social work contact and involvement
- Work with individuals, families, carers, groups and communities to help them make informed decisions
- Assess needs and options to recommend the course of action

Key Role 2: Plan, carry out, review and evaluate social work practice with individuals, families, carers, groups, communities and other professionals

- Interact with individuals, families, carers, groups and communities to achieve change and development and to improve life opportunities
- Prepare, produce, implement and evaluate plans with individuals, families, carers, groups, communities and professional colleagues

Key Role 5: Manage and be accountable with supervision and support for your own social work practice within your organisation

- Manage and be accountable for your own work

Key Role 6: Demonstrate professional competence in social work practice

- within agreed standards of social work practice and ensure your own professional development

It will also introduce you to the following academic standards as set out in the social work subject benchmark statement:

3.1.1 Social work services and service users

- The social processes (associated with, for example, poverty, unemployment, poor health, disablement, lack of education and other sources of disadvantage) that lead to marginalisation, isolation and exclusion and their impact on the demand for social work services
- The nature and validity of different definitions of, and explanations for, the characteristics and circumstances of service users and the services required by them

3.1.4 Social work theory

- Research-based concepts and critical explanations from social work theory and other disciplines that contribute to the knowledge base of social work, including their distinctive epistemological status and application to practice
- The relevance of psychological and physiological perspectives to understanding individual and social development and functioning

The subject skills highlighted to demonstrate this knowledge in practice include:

3.1.5 The nature of social work practice
- The nature and characteristics of skills associated with effective practice, both direct and indirect, with a range of service users and in a variety of settings including group care

3.2.2   Problem-solving skills

3.2.22   Gathering information

3.2.2.3 Analysis and synthesis

3.2.2.4 Intervention and evaluation

5.2.1   Knowledge and understanding
- Ability to use this knowledge and understanding in work within specific practice contexts

Introduction

In this chapter you will continue to explore specific areas of practice definitions, explanations, characteristics and related social work practice with older people who have specific needs. This chapter will consider the experience of older people with sensory impairments and physical impairments and how these needs are defined and the social work processes of engaging older people in assessment, planning, intervention and review can take account of their specific experiences and needs. Throughout each section of the chapter you will be encouraged to consider the links to social work practice.

This chapter is written in three parts. In the first part, you will explore the specific practice context of sensory impairment in older adults. Similarly, in the second part of the chapter you will examine the context of social work practice with older adults who have physical impairments and multiple impairments. As you move into the third section of the chapter you will draw together your learning from the first two parts to consider the specific social work skills, methods and services that are associated with effective practice with older people whose lives are affected by sensory, physical or multiple impairments. The final section of the chapter summarises your learning from the chapter.

Definitions

In this chapter we refer to sensory 'impairment' and physical 'impairment'.

ACTIVITY **5.1**

Define the term 'impairment' and the term 'disability'. What are the distinctions between each of the meanings?

The definition we have used for 'impairment' refers to '... lacking part of a limb, or having a defective limb, organism or mechanism of the body' – in effect the functional limitations that affect individual older people. A definition of 'disability' refers to '... the disadvantage or restriction of activity caused by a contemporary organisation which takes no or little account of people who have physical impairments and thus excludes them from the mainstream of social activity' (UPIAS, 1976). The distinction is that 'impairment' refers to and recognises the functional limitations that affect older people. The term 'disability' suggests that it is society's reaction to the older person's impairment that results in oppression and discrimination.

In chapter 4 and later in this chapter you will look at the social model of disability. You may recognise the underpinning premise of this model in the definition discussed above.

Older people and sensory impairment

In discussing issues related to older people with sensory impairment we are defining the term sensory impairment to mean older people who have hearing impairment and/or sight impairment.

Terminology

In order to develop your understanding of social work practice with older people who have sensory impairment, you will need to understand how these notions are defined and explained. You will start by considering the prevalence of visual impairment and hearing impairment before examining definitions, conditions and practice issues.

Visual Impairment

According to figures produced by the Royal National Institute for the Blind (RNIB), (**www.rnib.org.uk**), 98 per cent of people aged over 65 wear glasses. Of all people registered as blind or partially sighted 90 per cent are over 60 years of age. Older people are significantly more likely to suffer eye diseases than any other age group, with many of these older people experiencing loss of sight significant enough to affect independent living.

RESEARCH SUMMARY

Prevalence and incidence of visual impairment in the United Kingdom

- *At 31 March 2003, the number of people who were registered as blind was 157,000.*

- *The number of people registered blind in the age groups 65–74 and 75 or over declined by around 2 per cent since 31 March 2000.*

- *At 31 March 2003 the number of people who were registered as partially sighted was 155,000.*

- *68 per cent of people on the partially sighted register are aged 75 years or over.*

- *It is estimated that only a quarter of people who are blind or partially sighted are registered.*

Source: ***www.rnib.org.uk***

As can be seen from these figures, visual impairment is an age-related condition. Increased life expectancy means that more people will experience sight loss (Vale and Smyth, 2002). When considering what these figures mean in terms of social work practice and services for older people, it may be suggested that visual impairment affects a significant number and has a consequent impact on their life experience. This is both through the experience of visual impairment by the individual older person, for example the impact on everyday living tasks, and through the way that society may discriminate against them.

'Blind', or 'severely sight impaired' (DoH, 2004) means a high degree of sight loss. This could vary between seeing much less than normal or seeing nothing at all. Only about 18 per cent of visually impaired people are totally blind with the majority being able to distinguish between light and dark. Partially sighted or 'moderately sight impaired' (DoH, 2004) means less severe loss of vision.

There are many causes of impaired vision such as genetic conditions, disease, accidents and deterioration. There are also many forms of impaired vision depending on the condition: some older people have no central vision; others have no side vision; others may see things as severe blurs and others may see patchworks of defined areas and blanks. Some older people may be able to read large print yet have difficulties in crossing a road.

Particular medical conditions can have an impact on vision. The four main conditions of visual impairment associated with older age are:

- macular degeneration;

- cataracts;

- glaucoma;

- diabetic retinopathy.

Macular degeneration is the most common eye condition in older people. It occurs when the central part of the retina becomes damaged; this causes distortion of straight lines and blank/dark spots in the centre of vision. While it is not painful and does not lead to total sight loss, it can make everyday activities, such as cooking, reading and recognising faces, difficult and potentially hazardous. Cataracts are a clouding of the lens inside the eye. This causes blurred and cloudy vision and an increase in dazzle and glare. They can affect all aspects of daily living. Over half of older people over 65 have some degree of cataracts, 90 per cent of which can be treated with surgery. Glaucoma is a group of conditions in which the optic nerve is damaged at the point where it leaves the eye. If detected early it is treatable. However, once the nerve is damaged this cannot be reversed. It causes blank patches in vision with these patches enlarging if not treated, leaving only a small part of the central vision. Diabetic retinopathy is a complication of diabetes, with older people with diabetes being more likely to develop sight problems. It is important to identify a sight problem as early as possible as the earlier it is detected the more likely it is to be halted or even cured. Regular eye health checks are an essential part of this process.

There are certain welfare benefits and services for visually impaired people, for example specific aids to help in daily living tasks. However, to receive certain types of benefits the older person will need to be formally registered as severely or partially sight impaired. Local authorities have a statutory duty under the National Assistance Act 1948 to maintain a confidential register of people who are severely sight impaired and of people who are partially sight impaired. While this may allow older people to qualify for certain benefits, registration is not a prerequisite for obtaining help from the social services, such as an assessment of need and the provision of services, for example home care. The RNIB (1997) estimate that only one in three people who are eligible to register have done so.

ACTIVITY **5.2**

You have been asked to visit Stan, aged 69, to undertake an assessment of his needs as his sight is deteriorating. Consider what some of your assumptions are about what these needs may be.

Clearly everyone's needs are unique and it is important not to make assumptions. These may have the effect of stereotyping or stigmatising an individual. An important part of any assessment is to listen to the older person's view of their situation. Nevertheless, in planning an intervention with an older person it is important that you consider what the issues may be that could be raised. This will help you with your planning prior to the visit; for example in having the correct information available and in framing the questions that will support your assessment of Stan's needs as he sees them. Important features of preparation include gaining information, for example from other professionals such as the older person's general practitioner or, if appropriate, from relatives and carers. Using personal supervision to prepare for and reflect on your approach will also support you. In the case of Stan, you may notice the impact of his visual impairment in his actions. He may have to move his head frequently to focus and may have difficulty in making eye contact, finding it difficult to identify objects, faces or colours. Stan may walk slowly as he may be bumping into objects. This lack of confidence may result in falls, which could contribute to his vulnerability as he may be more prone to hip fractures (Felson et al., 1989). His daily living tasks may be affected as he may find them difficult. For examples, he may spill food or drink. Alternatively Stan may eat his food cold to avoid the risks in cooking. Mail may be unopened or unanswered. Socially and culturally Stan may feel isolated as he comes to terms with his impairment. He may avoid reading, watching television, undertaking leisure pursuits, attending social groups and functions or his religious institution. A consequence of this may be that Stan is depressed. None, some or all of this may be true. The important thing is to remember that people are individuals with unique responses and needs but that they are people first.

You also need to consider the impact of the additional discrimination that Stan and other older people with visual impairments may encounter. In Chapter 1 we explored the issues related to age discrimination – 'ageism'. Older people with visual impairments also experience additional disadvantages. Two-thirds of all people with a visual impairment have an additional disability or serious health problem which increases the likelihood of them experiencing treatment that is unfair. Over 50 per cent of older people who are visually impaired live alone, of which the majority are women. Over 90 per cent of visually impaired older people live on less than half the average national income: this is a widely accepted definition. Although older people from black and ethic minority communities have a higher incidence of eye disease, services do not reach these groups.

RESEARCH SUMMARY

'Progress in Sight' outlines national standards of social for visually impaired adults. They provide a framework for benchmarking existing services and do develop services. There are 16 standards that are listed below with a brief explanation. A fuller explanation and details are given within the document.

- Standard 1: *Involving inpaired adults in developing standards – involvement and influence in the planning and operation of services.*

- Standard 2: *Planning services – developing a multi-agency service plan.*

- Standard 3: *Commissioning services – services are timely and appropriate.*

- Standard 4: *Managing services – services are well resourced, delivered promptly and monitored throughly.*

- Standard 5: *Managing the workforce – workforce planning and training to take account of the current and future needs of visually impaired adults.*

- Standard 6: *Resourcing services – maximum use of all resources from all sources.*

- Standard 7: *Making services more accessible – up-to-date and timely information in the format of their choice.*

- Standard 8: *reaching adults with newly diagnosed sight problems – adults are made aware of the services available and how to get help if they need it.*

- Standard 9: *Involving service users in developing care pathways – service users are involved in decisions about their care management and rehabilitation.*

- Standard 10: *Supporting carers – involving carers while respecting different and separate needs.*

- Standard 11: *Assessing individual needs – social care needs are identified and assessed by competent staff within an agreed timescale.*

- Standard 12: *Agreeing the care plan – service users are helped to draw up a care plan which describes how their eligible needs will be meet.*

- Standard 13: *Providing emotional support – counselling and emotional support.*

- Standard 14: *Training people for life – a multi-disciplinary rehabilitation programme.*

- Standard 15: *Equipping people for life – specialised equipment, aids and minor adaptations.*

- Standard 16: *Achieving continuous improvements to services – continuous improvement through quality management and best practice.*

Source: *Association of Directors of Social Services (October 2002):* **www.adss.org.uk**

Hearing Impairment

According to figures produced by the Royal National Institute for the Deaf (RNID) there are estimated to be about 9 million deaf and hard of hearing people in the UK. About 698,000 of these are severely or profoundly deaf, 450,000 of whom cannot hear well enough to use a voice telephone, even with equipment to make it louder. The numbers of people with hearing impairments are increasing as the number of older people rises.

RESEARCH SUMMARY

- *The total of adults over 16 years of age estimated to have mild/moderate deafness is 6,911,000. There are 4,930,000 people over 60 years of age who are estimated to have mild/moderate deafness. This represents 71 per cent of all adults with mild/moderate deafness.*

- *The total number of adults over 16 years of age estimated to have a severe/profound deafness is 577,000. There are 487,000 people over 60 years of age who are estimated to have severe/profound deafness. This represents 84 per cent of adults with mild/moderate deafness.*

- *The total number of adults over 16 years of age estimated to have all degrees of deafness is 7,488,000. There are 5,417,000 people over 60 years of age who are estimated to have all degrees of deafness. This represents 72 per cent of all adults with all degrees of deafness.*

Source: ***www.rnid.org.uk***

As you will have noted, hearing impairment, as does sight impairment, affects a significant number of older people. Most of the 9 million deaf and hard of hearing people in the UK have developed a hearing loss as they get older. Only about 2 per cent of young adults are deaf or hard of hearing. Around the age of 50 the proportion of deaf people begins to increase sharply. The implications for social workers is that having a hearing impairment has a significant impact on the quality of the older person's life and their experience of everyday living, including the ways in which as a consequence of their hearing impairment they may experience additional discrimination.

Hearing loss and deafness is usually measured by finding the quietest sounds someone can hear using tones with different frequencies. These are heard as different pitches. The person being tested is asked to respond when they can hear a tone. The tone is adjusted until they can just hear it – the threshold. Thresholds are measured in decibels of hearing level (dBHL). Anyone with a threshold of up to 20dBHL across all the frequencies is considered to have 'normal' hearing.

Definitions of hearing impairment

- *Mild deafness*. People with mild deafness have some difficulty following speech, mainly in noisy situations. The quietest sounds they can hear in their better ear average between 25 and 39 decibels.

- *Moderate deafness.* People with moderate deafness have difficulty in following speech without a hearing aid. The quietest sounds they can hear in their better ear average between 40 and 69 decibels.

- *Severe deafness* People with severe deafness rely a lot on lip-reading, even with a hearing aid. British Sign Language (BSL) may be their first or preferred language. The quietest sounds they can hear in their better ear average between 70 and 94 decibels.

- *Profound deafness.* People who are profoundly deaf communicate by lip-reading. BSL may be their first or preferred language. The quietest sounds they can hear in their better ear average 95 decibels **(www.rnid.org)**.

More men than women experience hearing loss; this is assumed to be linked to hearing impairment as a result of industrial related noise. However, for older people aged over 80 years the number of women with hearing impairments is higher; this is directly linked to the fact that women live longer.

In England people with hearing impairment can register on a voluntary basis with their local social services department. In 2001, only 194,840 people in England were so registered as deaf or hard of hearing **(www.doh.gov.uk)**. As the RNID estimates that there are more than 9 million people with hearing impairments in England, and 577,000 of them are severely or profoundly deaf, it is clear that the registers are a very poor indicator of the numbers of people who are hearing impaired. You will recall this was a similar position for people with sight impairment.

ACTIVITY 5.3

What do you think are the reasons that people who are eligible do not choose to register? How would you persuade a person who is visually impaired of the advantage of registration?

You have probably thought of several reasons why older people may not be registering. Some older people may not seek help in relation to their condition so are not accessing the range of professionals who can help and advise them. Some older people may be unaware of registration and its potential benefits for them. Older people may not wish to be 'labelled' – registration can have an 'emotional' impact on the person, for example in symbolising loss (of faculties) and being seen as 'different'. As with all impairments, older people may view their impairment as a medical issue and may not see the benefits of the range of support that can be offered in the social care sector. A clear benefit to registration is the potential access to specific benefits and resources. Another indirect benefit lies in helping the government and local authorities to gain a 'true' picture of the number of people in their area who are hearing and/or visually impaired. This can support the development of resources and planning of services. It also can support individuals and groups campaigning, for example for improvements to transport links, access to buildings and access to services, by providing an accurate account of the number of people who have hearing and/or visual impairment.

ACTIVITY **5.4**

Tariq, aged 72 is a muslim. He has been experiencing loss of his hearing for the last two years and is now registered as having mild deafness. Consider the issues he may face in relation to his hearing impairment.

The impact of loss of hearing on an individual can be profound. Socially Tariq may be unable to hear people properly and will feel isolated. He may not be able to hear the radio, television, telephone or doorbell. Everyday tasks such as shopping may be difficult as, for example, he may find walking to the shops difficult in relation to the traffic. Asking for things and hearing the reply may also be difficult. This can have an impact at an emotional level – Tariq may feel isolated and this could lead to low self-esteem. Tariq will also experience additional issues as he is a person with a hearing impairment from a minority ethnic group.

RESEARCH SUMMARY

The research of Ahmad et al. (1998) into services for older people with hearing impairments from ethnic minority groups found that services are organised around issues of cultural and religious identity and challenging marginalisation from white deaf organisations. Education, training and social support were being organised through informal networks. Alongside this, there was an increasing awareness of problems of access to and appropriateness of services among professionals. Approaches to provision, however, reflected an emphasis on short-termism and 'special needs'. Further, focus was largely on Asian and Afro-Carribbean deaf people and families. Hard-of-hearing, deafened and deaf-blind people were poorly served, as were deaf people from other groups. Though there were developments, they found little was changing in mainstream provision and developments were not based on a coherent strategy.

As with services for older people with visual impairments, national standards have been developed jointly by the Royal National Institute for the Deaf (RNID), the Association of Directors of Social Services (ADSS), the Local Government Association (LGA) and the Deaf Blind Association (DBA) – 'Best Practice Standards for Deaf and Hard of Hearing People' (July 1999). They were developed as a consequence of the publication of a report by the Social Services Inspectorate (SSI), *'A Service on the Edge'* (August 1997) following a national inspection of services for deaf and hard of hearing people which highlighted the variable standards and poor range of services.

RESEARCH SUMMARY

Best Practice Standards for Deaf and Hard of Hearing People (July 1999)

- Standard 1: *Information – distributing information that is accessible and appropriate to meet the needs of service users.*

- Standard 2: *Access to services – physical access, reception staff that are trained and other staff that are trained.*

- Standard 3: *Communcation services – communications services policy and procedure.*

- Standard 4: *Assessing and identifying appropriate services – meeting the specific needs of people with hearing impairment.*

- Standard 5: *Assessment and provision of specialised equipment.*

- Standard 6: *Accessible services at home and outside the home.*

- Standard 7: *Planning – with service users and others.*

- Standard 8: *Service procedures – to support the delivery of high-quality services.*

- Standard 9: *Procedures for joint working/managing responsibilty – between and with other agencies.*

Source: ***www.rnid.org.uk***

Physical and multiple impairments

Increased longevity suggests that the health of older people has improved. However, there are particular problems associated with being older which affect not only health but also long-term quality of life. Many older people have specific health needs that have implications for the provision of social work and community care services.

The main causes of disability in older age, following sight and hearing impairments, are arthritis, heart disease, chronic bronchitis, back problems and strokes (**www.ageconcern.org.uk**). In this section we are going to focus on two aspects of physical impairment identified in the NSF For Older People (DoH 2001a) – strokes and falls. The NSF identifies the need to reduce the incidence of strokes and, for those who have stroke, to receive access to integrated stroke care services (Standard 5). Standard 6 focuses on the need to reduce the number of falls and ensure effective treatment and rehabilitation for those who have a fall. The emphasis in these standards is on prevention and reduction of the impact of physical impairment.

Strokes

RESEARCH SUMMARY

- *It is estimated that each year in England and Wales 110,000 people have their first stroke, with 30,000 people having a further stroke. The vast majority of these numbers are older people.*

- *Strokes are single biggest cause of severe disabilty and the third most common cause of death in the UK and other developed countries.*

- *Around 30 per cent of people die in the first month after a stroke. After a year 65 per cent of people who survive a stroke can live independently, 35 per cent are significantly disabled and require considerable care. Around 5 per cent are admitted to long-term residential care.*

- *Substantial proportions of resources in health and social care are given to caring for people who have strokes.*

Source: NSF for Older People (DoH, 2001)

The most common cause of psychological problems among older people is strokes. Most strokes are blood clots that get stuck in the small blood vessels (capillaries) in the brain that supply neurons with oxygen and other necessities. There are two main types of strokes:

- *Ischaemic strokes* – when a blood clot narrows or blocks a blood vessel so blood cannot reach the brain. When this happens, many neurons die for lack of oxygen. This is the most common form of stroke. Transient ischaemic attacks (TIAs) are described as 'mini strokes' and symptoms and signs resolve within 24 hours; however, TIA's increase the chance of strokes.

- *Haemorrhagic stroke* – when a blood vessel bursts and blood leaks into the brain causing damage.

The effect of the stroke depends on the part of the brain that has been damaged as well as the older person's health at the time. It can affect walking, talking, eating, writing, care of self – a whole range of skills. There is no preventative treatment for strokes other than controlling blood pressure which, along with age, is the major risk factor. Factors such as smoking, drinking and diabetes also contribute to the problem. Physical, occupational and speech therapy can help older people who have experienced strokes regain much of what they have lost by re-learning or learning to work around abilities or skills they have lost.

ACTIVITY 5.5

Christine aged 84, was admitted to hospital two weeks ago following a major stroke. Staff on the ward are very concerned about her as she appears to be very unhappy, rarely speaking. You have been asked to speak to her. Consider why Christine may be unhappy. What could you do to reassure her?

We acknowledge that we have only given you limited information from which to make your assumptions; you would want to gain a fuller picture of the person from, for example, those involved in her care. Additionally you will recognise the need not to make assumptions about a person without talking to them. You should listen to what the service user says and thinks without jumping to any conclusions. Nevertheless in preparing for any contact with an older person, part of your preparation is to consider your own thoughts and feelings, how you would seek to engage Christine in a meaningful dialogue and how you would address some of the issues which may be raised. In considering Christine's unhappiness, you could have considered the direct link to the consequences of having had a stroke. Her unhappiness and lack of communication may be a reflection of Christine's feelings of low self-esteem and self-worth; she may feel like a burden, unsure of her future. She may feel totally dependent for her care on others and see the future as one of dependency rather than independence. Often older people feel let down, out of control and not able to have a say about what is happening to them. They may feel as if they have been swallowed up by the system and are powerless to do anything about it. In seeking to engage Christine in a dialogue it is important that you give her time and space to express herself and what she may be feeling. You should ensure that you provide Christine with any answers to questions and with any information that she requires. These may include talking to her about the assessment process: what is involved, its purpose and, importantly, how Christine herself will be centrally involved. The older person and their family are at the centre of any processes and should be allowed to direct and feel they are in charge wherever possible. You will need to explain your role and the way you work with other professionals. If you make any promises to her, carry them out. If you cannot do something that Christine asks of you tell her what and who may be able to help her. If you will be visiting again, ensure that you keep the agreed contact.

Falls

According to the NSF for Older People (DoH, 2001) falls are a major cause of disability and the leading cause of mortality due to injury in older people aged over 75 in the UK.

RESEARCH SUMMARY

- *Over 400,000 older people a year attend Accident and Emergency departments following an accident.*

- *Hip fractures are the most common serious injury related to falls in older people.*

- *14,000 people a year in the UK die as a result of an osteoporotic hip fracture.*

- *One in three women and one in 12 men over 50 are affected by osteoporosis.*

- *Almost half of all women experience an osteoporotic fracture by the time they reach 70.*

- *After an osteoporotic hip fracture, 50 per cent of people can no longer live independently.*

Source: *NSF for Older People (DoH, 2001)*

Osteoporosis is a condition caused by a reduction in bone mass and density, therefore increasing the risk of fractures when an older person falls. The most common places to have a fracture are the hip, spine and wrist.

One focus on averting falls should be on prevention. This involves recognising those people who are most at risk such as older people with visual or physical impairment or mobility problems associated with medical conditions such as Parkinson's disease. Risk factors may also occur in the home; examples include poor lighting, steep stairs and loose carpets.

ACTIVITY 5.6

Consider the impact on the following older people of a fall:
- *John, aged 87, no longer cares for himself. He is depressed and unhappy and spends his time sitting in a chair staring out of the window.*

- *Eleanor shuffles when she walks, clinging to the furniture.*

- *Beryl was always independent. She now depends on her daughter to do all her cleaning, shopping and cooking*

- *Daphne lies at the bottom of the stairs. It is now early evening and she has been there since this morning. She is too frightened to get up. She is very cold and tired. Although she has been shouting out, nobody comes.*

These case studies are intended to illustrate the potential psychological impact on an older person of and after a fall. In John's case his loss of mobility has led to depression and consequent social isolation. Eleanor appears to have lost her confidence about moving around safely. Beryl's fall has resulted in an increase in dependency. Appropriate professional intervention, rehabilitation and support could be used to help these older people. This will require intervention by a range of professionals such as health and social care workers which will need to be carefully planned and co-ordinated. These issues are discussed further in Chapter 7. Daphne appears to be suffering from the beginnings of hypothermia. Older people who are at risk of falling or have fallen should be assessed and reviewed regularly to monitor their needs. This may include longer-term emotional and social support to maximise independence and to prevent social isolation and depression.

Multiple impairments

There is increasing concern about older people who are visually and hearing impaired. It is estimated that for every one person under 50 that is visually and hearing impaired, there are ten times as many people who are visually and hearing impaired over 80 years of age – 23,000 people under the age of 70 and 24,000 people over the age of 80 (**www.sense.org.uk**).

Developing adequate and effective services for older people with multiple impairments is a major challenge (McDonald, 1999). The emphasis must be on supporting older people with multiple impairments and developing services that support normalisation – integration and participation into normal activities. As McDonald (1999) suggests: 'The professional must change from being the expert definer of need and rationer of services to being a resource which the disabled person may use as he or she chooses' (page 227).

In the first part of the chapter you have looked at the experience of sensory impairment on the lives of older people. You have also considered the experience of physical impairment through using two examples that affect the lives of some older people in our society, strokes and falls. You have considered the prevalence of such impairments among older people and have considered how these disabilities may impact on the lives of older people. Having developed your knowledge in respect of these specific areas of social work practice, in the next part of the chapter you will build on learning from this chapter and from Chapter 4 to support your reflections on your individual approach to engaging and working with people with impairments.

Social work practice with older people

In Chapter 4 and in this chapter we have outlined the standards that services should use to respond effectively to individual needs. In terms of social work practice, we have examined how this is effected through the core social work processes of assessment, planning, intervention, monitoring and review. We have also stressed the importance of a multi-disciplinary approach. In this section you will build on this learning to consider what are the skills that older service users and their families want and how we take these into account when assessing, planning and providing services to older people with impairments.

Impairment in older age is often perceived as the inevitable consequence of growing older. The danger with this assumption is that the impairment is not seen as 'genuine', merely a factor of age. Having an impairment has a profound effect on personal well-being and, as we have seen in Chapter 1, at the social, cultural and institutional level. This may result in the effect of the disability not being taken into account in the older person's care plan, the impact of which may be that the person does not get the specialised help they require to increase their independence, such as mobility training. This is compounded for older people from black and ethnic minority groups as services may not specifically target these groups or take into account their specific needs (Ahmed and Cheeseman, 1996).

You will recall in Chapter 4 you examined the individual and social models of disability. While examples were given in that chapter in relation to older people with mental health needs and older people with learning disability, these theoretical models should also be examined in relation to the experience of all older people with impairments.

The dominant response from the disabled people's movement is, rather than be seen as passive victims, to organise together through their common experience to effect change. Barnett (2002) suggests that older people with impairments would suffer their disability as an 'experience' rather than part of the 'cultural understanding' of younger disabled people. The implication here is that people who are born with impairments or develop an impairment in younger adulthood are more likely to be aware of and part of the disability movement, which emphasises the culture and independence of people who are disabled. This emphasises the way in which society impairs people. However, as Means et al. (2002: 169) suggest:

> *Whilst disabled people themselves have been largely responsible for the theoretical advances in the understanding of disability, older people have played no such role in the study of ageing and thus have been distanced not only from the insights of the disability movement but from equivalent developments relating to old age.*

Older people find themselves outside this culture of disability, further isolating them and their experience of impairment. The social model of disability provides a good starting point; drawing on psychological and sociological aspects and a narrative account of disability provides a more holistic understanding and acknowledges the reality of the impact of the impairment and disability for the older person (Tregaskis, 2002; Marks, 1999).

ACTIVITY **5.6**

As you read the following case, consider what your thoughts and feelings are.

You have been asked to undertake an assessment of Don, aged 77, following a referral by his general practitioner. Don lives with his wife, Anna, aged 78, in a pleasant part of the town in a small bungalow. His daughter and grandson live nearby and his son lives 100 miles away. Don was a professional engineer in industry until his retirement at the age of 68. Since then he has continued to have an active life, for example maintaining the home and garden, undertaking voluntary work for two days a week and taking a number of holidays with his family. Don has recently suffered a stroke; two years ago he had a heart attack. He also has a hearing and sight impairment as a result of the long-term impact of his job in the engineering sector. His General Practitioner feels that Don and his wife might be able to benefit from some support and services. He stated that Don is very reluctant to meet with 'a social worker'.

In thinking about this case you may have identified a number of thoughts and feelings. These may have focused on what you believe the purpose of your visit and the tasks to be in visiting Don and his wife Anna. These could include concerns about how you will be received by them. Why may Don be very reluctant for you to visit? This could be linked to views about being assessed for and receiving services – being seen to be dependent on services as opposed to independent. Despite the legitimate rights of older people to receive services, some older people may feel that accessing services is demeaning and regarded as taking control away from them. You may be speculating on Don and Anna's expectations for and from your visit. This could have led you into thinking about how you could engage the couple in a meaningful dialogue about Don's needs, and Anna's needs as the main carer. Engaging the older person, their carers and their families in a meaningful dialogue must be a critical process.

Studies on what service users want from social workers emphasise the importance of the personal qualities of the individual demonstrated through a professional approach (McDonald, 1999). These include reliability, empathy, good listening skills and efficiency. Smale and Tuson (1993) outline an exchange model of assessment in which the older person is an equal partner in the assessment of their need. Developing a partnership based on participation with the older person will be an essential feature of this. Marsh and Fisher (1992) suggest that the general principles of partnership are to work through negotiated agreement and with the explicit consent of the service user; where this is not in place involvement should be kept to the minimum. This must be seen in the context of statutory responsibilities, for example concerns about abuse. These are outlined in Chapters 3 and 6. Further, Marsh and Fisher (1992) suggest that service users must have the greatest possible degree of choice in the services that they may be offered. What this means in practice is that the role of the worker needs to focus on ways in which you can be a resource for the older person to use in reaching their own goals rather than employing an approach which emphasises the 'management'of the older person. The suggestion that workers with older people should become a resource to be used by older people is not a suggestion that professionals should become passive and all the responsibility, for example for assessment, planning, decision-making and innovations in practice, should now rest with the older person. Rather, what is being suggested is that workers acting as a resource to be used by others need to use skills that promote control by older people and older people with impairments. To promote something is to take an active role and, in this case, an active role in helping older people learn how to use professionals as a resource in solving the goals of rehabilitation. To do this professional workers will need to use skills, such as empowerment, participation and the promotion of rights and responsibilities, and practice which recognises diversity and difference. In all of this the worker needs to learn how to listen to older people while at the same time helping the older person to identify the central issues. Is it, for example, important to learn to use a wheelchair or to lip read? Or is it firstly important to isolate the purpose of these activities and encourage older people with impairments to find the most appropriate solutions that will enable them to be independent in meeting their own needs? The need is for a meaningful dialogue and relationship to develop between the older person and those involved in their care.

In this part of the chapter you have developed your knowledge in respect of social work practice and services related to work with older people with impairments. As stated earlier, all of the skills and processes that are characteristic of good social work practice are relevant to work with older people and their carers. In this part of the chapter we have focused on some of the interpersonal skills that support effective practice with older people and older people who experience impairments.

C H A P T E R S U M M A R Y

This chapter has, as in Chapter 4, focused on helping you to meet the social work subject benchmark 3.1.1, which requires you to understand 'The nature and validity of different definitions of, and explanations for, the characteristics and circumstances of service users [in this case, older people] and the services required by them'. You have achieved this by reading and working through activities that explore definitions, theoretical explanations, characteristics and related social work practice with older people who experience sensory and physical impairments. The chapter started by looking separately at issues related to older people with sensory impairments and issues related to older people with physical impairments. In the last section we have given you an opportunity to consider the range of interpersonal skills of social work and the values of social work practice with older people with impairments.

FURTHER READING

McDonald, A. (1999) *Understanding Community Care.* Basingstoke: Palgrave Macmillan.
While this book is not specifically on the needs of older people with impairments, it does have a chapter which explores specific issues for adults with particular needs. It also offers an insight into all aspects of assessment and planning for community care services.

WEBSITES

www.rnib.orr.uk
This site contains a wealth of information about visual impairment that is easily accessible to all people. All information is available in a variety of media.

www.seeability.org
See Ability's aim is to enable individuals who are visually impaired and have additional disabilities to achieve their full potential.

www.rnid.org.uk
This site contains a wealth of information about hearing impairments and is accessible to all people. All information is available in a variety of media.

www.britishdeafassociation.org.uk
This is the largest UK charity run for and by deaf people for people who use sign language.

www.sense.org.uk
Sense is an organisation for people who are deaf-blind or have associated disabilities.

Chapter 6
Vulnerability and abuse

The subject skills highlighted to demonstrate this knowledge in practice include:

3.2.2   Problem-solving skills

3.2.2.1 Managing problem-solving activities

3.2.2.2 Gathering information

3.2.2.3 Analysis and synthesis

3.2.2.4 Intervention and evaluation

3.2.3   Communication skills

- Listen actively to others, engage appropriately with the life experiences of service users, understand accurately their viewpoint and overcome personal prejudices to respond appropriately to a range of complex personal and interpersonal situations

3.2.4 Skills in working with others

- Involve users of social work services in ways that increase their resources, capacity and power to influence factors affecting their lives;
- Consult actively with others, including service users, who hold relevant information or expertise;
- Act co-operatively with others, liaising and negotiating across differences such as organisational and professional boundaries and differences of identity or language

5.2.1 Knowledge and understanding

- Ability to use this knowledge and understanding in work within specific practice contexts

Introduction

The focus of this chapter will be the concepts of vulnerability, abuse, risks and rights in relation to social work practice with older people. While these notions will be found throughout the whole book, this chapter seeks to explore them specifically and in greater depth, and in doing so will enable you to develop your understanding and skills in working with vulnerable older people who may experience abusive situations.

In this chapter you will start by reading a brief outline of the historical context of vulnerability and abuse in respect of older adults. You will then study some of the terms that are used to describe abusive situations and particular types of abuse, including a consideration of how these terms have adapted and changed over time. The chapter will also draw your attention to the legal and political context of these notions through, in particular, an examination of the national policy document on Protection for Vulnerable Adults, *No Secrets: Guidance on developing and implementing multi-agency policies and procedures to protect vulnerable adults from abuse* (DoH, 2000a).

In the last two sections of this chapter you will explore direct social work practice related to the relevant processes and skills involved in the identification, investigation and prevention of abuse. This will include consideration of the user perspective and the professional dilemmas that result from potential contradictions presented by the perceived need for protection and the social work value of enhancing self-determination.

Historical Context

Throughout this book we have presented the theme of continuity and change. We would suggest that the historical context of what we now term *abuse of vulnerable adults* can also be explained through the theme of continuity and change. We do not, therefore, intend to give you a detailed history of developments in respect of issues of adult abuse.

We will, however, demonstrate that this is not a new phenomenon; rather it is one that has only come to the attention of professionals and the general public in the past 25–30 years.

Biggs et al. (1995) suggest that the historical context of the care of older people is 'bound up with the history of the poor and the varied experiences of those without an independent income' (page 9). This argument is supported by a closer examination of demographic trends; household structures and the status of older people in society, illustrating that up to the late 1950s older people mostly lived within large families or isolated institutions where issues were silent and hidden. It was not until the 1960s and 1970s that families became dispersed and divided with greater numbers of older people living alone or in small residential or community establishments (Biggs et al., 1995). Furthermore, it was about another decade, in the 1970s and early 1980s, before the notion of maltreatment of older people began to be recognised and given a name and definition. Clearly, just because it had not previously been acknowledged does not mean that it did not exist; conversely, it is likely that because there was no known categorisation of the issue, it was not identified.

Gradually over many years, the notion that in this society older people were being subjected to different forms of abuse began to be documented and accepted. Then, following consultation, in March 2000 the Department of Health issued national guidance, *No Secrets: Guidance on developing and implementing multi-agency policies and procedures to protect vulnerable adults from abuse* (DoH, 2000a). This document represents a significant development in the recognition and identification of adult abuse. You will be examining this in much more detail as you progress through this chapter. In the next section you will examine the terminology commonly used to describe key concepts in this area of practice, including a historical look at how these terms have developed.

Terminology

Taking a historical perspective also provides you with an insight into the range of words and phrases that have been used to describe the complex issues that are the focus of this chapter. Biggs et al. (1995) provide a useful 'chronological development of terminology' in this area, concluding at the time that the term 'elder abuse' was a favoured phrase that had 'managed the test of time' (page 36). However, in more recent years, while the term 'abuse' remains in use, the more generic phrase 'vulnerable adult' appears to have replaced 'elder', thereby removing the age differentiation and encompassing all adults. The following summary includes and updates the work of Biggs et al.

RESEARCH SUMMARY

Granny battering *(Baker, 1975)*

Elder abuse *(O'Malley et al., 1979)*

The battered elder syndrome *(Block and Sinnott, 1979)*

Elder mistreatment and vulnerable adults *(Douglass et al., 1980)*

Granny bashing *(Eastman and Sutton, 1982)*

Old age abuse *(Eastman, 1984)*

▶

Inadequate care of the elderly *(Fulmer and O'Malley, 1987)*

Granny abuse *(Eastman, 1988)*

Mis-care *(Hocking, 1988)*

Elder abuse *(DoH, 1992)*

The abuse of older people *(Pritchard, 1995)*

Adult protection *(DoH, 2000a)*

Abuse of vulnerable adults *(DoH, 2000a; Pritchard, 2001)*

Developed from Biggs et al. (1995)

You will see how the terms 'adult', 'vulnerable' and 'abuse' are currently considered the most appropriate terms, particularly as they feature in the national guidance *No Secrets* (DoH, 2000a). Later in this chapter you will examine the national guidance in detail. Firstly, though, in order to fully understand the concepts of *vulnerability* and *abuse*, we will explore them further before moving on to consider the legal and policy framework to social work practice with older people who are deemed to be *vulnerable adults* at risk of *abuse*.

ACTIVITY 6.1

Think about the term 'vulnerable' and what it means to you.

- *Write down your own definition of 'vulnerable'.*
- *Make a list of adults that you know who you consider to be 'vulnerable'.*
- *Have you ever felt 'vulnerable'? Make a note of when this was, why you felt 'vulnerable' and what it felt like.*

As with many words in the English language the notion of vulnerability is not a straightforward one. The definition of 'vulnerable adult' used by the Department of Health goes back to the consultation paper issued by the Lord Chancellor's Department in 1997, *Who Decides?* The same definition is used within the *No Secrets* document (DoH, 2000a). A 'vulnerable adult' is a person:

Who is or may be in need of community care services by reason of mental or other disability, age or illness; and

Who is or may be unable to take care of him or herself, or unable to protect him or herself against significant harm or exploitation. (DoH, 2000a: 8–9)

If you look up the word 'vulnerable' in a dictionary or thesaurus, however, you will find synonyms such as: susceptible, weak, dependent, defenceless, helpless, in danger, exposed. Therefore the meanings attached to vulnerability could be seen to be linked to negative concepts that include notions of powerlessness. Additionally, as you saw in the chronology of terms, the word 'protection' has also been evident in more recent documentation. *Protection* and *vulnerability* could be seen to be in complete opposition to the social work values of *autonomy*, *respect* and *empowerment*. You will explore this debate further within this chapter, particularly when you consider the importance of the user perspective towards the end of the chapter.

In Activity 6.1, you were also asked to make a list of people that you know and would consider to be vulnerable. It is likely that there are some common factors about the people that you have listed. You may recognise some of these aspects within the points below, which are all features that are known to increase the risk of abuse taking place:

- The person is socially isolated with limited social contacts, probably lives alone and has few visitors.

- The person has poor health or a disability and is dependent upon others for some level of support in order to meet their daily living needs. This may be practical, financial or emotional support.

- There have been one or more previous incidents of abuse taking place towards that person. These may be as a result of a long-term relationship difficulty or may be abuse perpetrated by persons unknown to the injured party.

As you undertook the activity, you then considered whether you had ever felt vulnerable. It would be most unusual if you could not think of many instances when this was the case. Examples might include: when out alone in the dark; being unable to find your way around a large city; a time when you were not well, perhaps after an operation. Whatever your examples were, the common feelings will most probably encompass lack of control, being at a disadvantage, being exposed or threatened in some way.

You will see from this activity that everyone can experience vulnerability – people may feel vulnerable for short periods of time and there are degrees of vulnerability. The notion is further complicated by subjectivity. In other words, the state of vulnerability and the degree of risk may be felt or perceived differently by different people in the same situation. Equally, the risks that are known to be present may not correspond with the person's perception of their vulnerability. This mismatch of understanding in a situation can be apparent in different ways: the individual may feel highly vulnerable without apparent foundation for their fears; or the individual may feel secure and in no way vulnerable where others would perceive great risk. Throughout this book, we have highlighted the importance of listening to the individual and the meanings that they attach to their circumstances. Social work practice with older people, who may be vulnerable to abuse, is no different and needs to take careful, accurate account of the older person's views, their personal history in their own words and their perceptions of what is going on around them. Through your consideration of Activity 6.1 and the comments above, you have developed your understanding of the complex term *vulnerability*. The other term which we found used commonly in current literature, policy and guidance is *abuse*.

ACTIVITY 6.2

Think about the term 'abuse'.

- Write down your own definition of 'abuse'.

- Make a list of different situations that you would consider 'abusive'.

You may not have found it easy to come to a succinct and clear definition of 'abuse'. In reality the word is open to a variety of interpretations and meanings. We would expect that your definition includes some of the following words and phrases: harm, injure, violate, neglect, exploit, mistreat, insult, take advantage of. The Department of Health provides a definition of abuse in *No Secrets*:

> *Abuse is a violation of an individual's human and civil rights by any other person or persons. (DoH, 2000a: 9)*

The *No Secrets* document goes on to explain how abuse may only happen on one occasion, or may be characterised by repeated violations. Furthermore, abuse is then categorised into six different types (DoH, 2000a: 9).

Anna lives in a care home for older people. Anna has fallen many times recently, often sustaining injuries. She is restless and does not like sitting down for long periods. The care staff are very concerned about the risk that Anna will fall again if she walks around alone. Now, if they notice Anna starting to rise from her chair, they will manually move her back down into a sitting position and, whilst talking to her, gently hold her down, until they feel the impetus to stand up has passed.

Barbara lives in an extra-care housing complex where she receives support. She has her own flat but likes to go into the common-room area to sit and talk with other people. One morning, whilst she was in the common room alone, a man who also lives in the complex, came into the common room, undid his trousers and exposed himself to her.

Colin lives in the same house that he was born in 76 years ago. He lives with his only son, Peter, who is 38 years old. For many years Peter has misused alcohol and other substances. He does not have paid employment but is often not at home for long periods. When he returns home, Colin is frightened. Peter can be verbally aggressive, he will shout and swear and frequently threatens Colin with violence, although he has never physically hurt him.

Douglas lives with his niece, Lisa, and her husband in their period cottage, set in a tourist village in Devon. Douglas has no children of his own, he has always thought of his niece as being like a daughter. Fifteen years ago when he was widowed, he sold his own house and gave the money to Lisa so that she could buy the cottage. He now lives and spends most of his time in a small annex attached to the cottage. Douglas gets very lonely, but understands that Lisa and her husband need time together; he does not get upset when they lock the door to his annex area so that they can eat their meals or sit together without interruption from Douglas.

Elizabeth and Emily are sisters and both are over 80 years of age. They live together but both have learning difficulties so provide mutual support. Elizabeth is more able than Emily, particularly where household organisation, shopping and finances are concerned. Recently a home care support worker noted that whilst Elizabeth had been eating a good and varied diet, she had not been ensuring that there was enough food in the home for her sister. Emily had lost weight and appeared to be dehydrated. Emily had rummaged through the worker's bag, seemingly looking for food or drink.

Iman is an 80-year-old black man. He is a Muslim. He lives in his own home within a largely white community in middle England. Iman has recently approached local services for assistance to prepare meals, because arthritis is restricting his mobility and dexterity. Following the appropriate assessment, it was agreed that a frozen meals service would be provided to meet Iman's needs. However, when the choice of meals was made known to Iman, it was apparent that none of the choices met his religious, cultural or dietary needs. He therefore refused to receive the service.

ACTIVITY 6.3

Read the six case vignettes above. For each situation:

- *Do you think that this situation would be considered as abuse?*

- *If so, what type of abuse may be happening?*

Each of these case vignettes would warrant further investigation, but there are indications that abuse may be occurring. In each example a different form of abuse may be evident. In Table 6.1 we explain the categories of abuse (DoH, 2000a: 9) and give examples of the acts that would be considered within that form of abuse.

Table 6.1 Forms of abuse

	Definition	Examples (Developed from *No Secrets*, DoH, 2000a)
Physical abuse	Physical abuse is actual or threatened touching which the recipient has not consented to and which may cause pain or harm to the person.	Hitting, scratching, slapping, pushing, kicking, burning, misuse of medication (too much or too little), restraint, rough handling, involuntary isolation, inappropriate sanctions.
Sexual abuse	'Sexual acts or physical contact without consent or where the vulnerable adult was not able to consent or was pressured into consent' (DoH, 2000a: 9).	Rape, indecent exposure, sexual assault, making inappropriate suggestions verbally or physically.
Psychological abuse	'... when an older person suffers mental anguish as a result ... psychological abuse is usually characterized by a pattern of behaviour repeated over time and intended to maintain a hold of fear over the older person' (Pritchard, 2001: 100).	Emotional abuse, threats of harm or abandonment, deprivation of contact, bullying, humiliation, blaming, controlling, intimidation, emotional blackmail, coercion, harassment, verbal abuse, shouting, swearing, isolation or withdrawal from services or supportive networks, denial of human rights such as privacy, choice and dignity.
Financial or material abuse	'The illegal or improper exploitation and/or use of funds or materials' (Biggs et al., 1995).	Theft, fraud, exploitation, pressure in connection with wills, property, inheritance or financial transactions, preventing access or control of assets, or the misuse or misappropriation of property, possessions or benefits

Neglect and acts of omission	Neglect is the failure to ensure that necessary care is provided. This can be physical and/or emotional, it may be intentional or may be due to lack of knowledge or skill on the abuser's part.	Ignoring medical or physical care needs, failure to provide access to appropriate health, social care or education services, withholding the necessities of life, including medication, nutrition and heating. Refusal to allow others to provide necessary care, failure to report suspicions that abuse is taking place in a care setting.
Discriminatory abuse	Inequality of opportunity or actions based on a person's race, gender, age, sexuality, disability, culture or religion.	Racism, sexism, harassment, slurs, exclusion, isolation, denying access to provision of services, lack of respect or inappropriate use of language.

It is important to note that individual abusive situations cannot always be classified in straightforward categories as this might suggest. However, understanding the possible forms of abuse can help social workers to identify, assess and describe the particular issues that arise in each situation.

The potential risk of these different forms of abuse of vulnerable older people occurring is known to be present in all settings: in the community, living alone, with informal or formal carers, in supported living environments, in institutional settings such as care establishments and hospitals (Biggs, 1995; DoH, 2000a; Ryan, 2001; Sumner, 2002). Furthermore, 'vulnerable adult(s) may be abused by a wide range of people including relatives and family members, professional staff, paid care workers, volunteers, other service users, neighbours, friends and associates, people who deliberately exploit vulnerable people and strangers' (DoH, 2000a: 10). However, earlier in the chapter you read about some of the known features that may increase the vulnerability of the older person, in a similar way, there are certain traits that characterise abusers. Kurrle (2001: 97) describes the 'abuser psychopathology', that is the individual, personal characteristics that may be a factor in the person becoming an abuser. Significant factors listed by Kurrle include alcoholism, drug abuse, psychiatric illness and cognitive impairment. Following this, Kurrle also acknowledges the complex dimensions of *family dynamics*, including family history and domestic violence, and *carer stress* as further potential contributing factors.

Legal and Policy Context

In the previous section of this chapter, we have concentrated on the meanings of key terms and concepts; in particular you have been considering what is understood by the words *vulnerable adults* and *abuse*. You have also read about the different forms of abuse and considered some of the predisposing factors that may lead to an abusive situation. In this section you will explore how social care related laws and policies provide a contextual framework for professional practice with vulnerable older people. In Chapter 3 of this book, you examined the significance of legislative frameworks, policy directives and service delivery standards on social work practice with all older people. In this chapter, your studies will be more specifically focused on the legal and policy context of social work practice with older adults considered to be vulnerable and at risk of, or experiencing, abuse.

As you have seen in earlier parts of this chapter, there is evidence of increasing awareness and concern about the prevalence of abuse of older people in our society. In 2003 a House of Commons Select Committee began an inquiry into this issue and in their report, which was published in April 2004, a range of proposals that will impact upon health and social care services was announced. However, currently the national government guidance document *No Secrets* (DoH, 2000a) is the most significant national document that addresses the recognition and management of abuse of older people. In this section of the chapter we will start by discussing this guidance.

No Secrets: Guidance on developing and implementing multi-agency policies and procedures to protect vulnerable adults from abuse (DoH, 2000a)

In this chapter so far, we have mentioned the current national guidance *No Secrets* document many times. While the *No Secrets* document has the status of a Code of Practice rather than statute or primary law, it was issued under Section 7 of the Local Authority Social Services Act 1970. This means that it is *statutory guidance* and it must be implemented and adhered to in the same way as if it were set as a piece of legislation in its own right (Johns and Sedgwick, 1999). You should also note that this document does not only refer to older people but also provides a *framework for action* across all adults who fall within its definitions.

In the *No Secrets* guidance, the Department of Health starts out by looking at issues of definition, as we have done in this chapter. The four sections that make up the main part of the document focus on the creation of multi-agency administrative frameworks, policies, strategies and procedures for the protection from abuse of vulnerable adults. The final section briefly outlines ways in which information about local multi-agency arrangements can be disseminated both within agencies and to the wider public.

RESEARCH SUMMARY

No Secrets: Guidance on developing and implementing multi-agency policies and procedures to protect vulnerable adults from abuse (DoH, 2000a)

Section 1 – Introduction
Outlines some of the background and key purposes of the document, including a stress on partnership approaches and coherent strategies. The structure of the document is also outlined in this section.

Section 2 – Defining who is at risk and in what way
In order to assist agencies to clarify definitions both locally and nationally, this section considers definitions and understandings of: vulnerable adult; abuse; institutional abuse; who may be the abuser; the circumstances of abuse; patterns of abusing; the justification for intervention; issues of assessment.

Section 3 – Setting up an inter-agency framework
Section 3 starts out by designating the local authority social services as the lead agency but then takes the reader through the steps required to create an inter-agency framework which includes all the relevant local agencies.

Section 4 – Developing inter-agency policy

In looking at how inter-agency policy should be developed, this section lays out the guiding principles of such policies.

Section 5 – Main elements of the strategy

As 'a long-term plan for implementing policy' (page 22) the key components of a local strategy are listed in this section. Associated issues such as training, purchasing and contracting services, and confidentiality are also addressed within this section.

Section 6 – Procedures for responding in individual cases

In section 6, the detail of how inter-agency local procedures should address responses to allegations of adult abuse and the resultant processes are provided. Thus investigation, record-keeping, assessment and related procedures are covered.

Section 7 – Getting the message across

The last section of No Secrets *takes a different focus, in that it explores how information, philosophies and broader guidance can be circulated within, across and outside of the agencies involved.*

Therefore *No Secrets* set in place some fundamental requirements: that local multi-agency guidelines and procedures be put in place; that within a multi-agency approach, social services would be the lead agency; that each area would set up an Adult Protection Committee; and that this committee would produce an annual report. Thus as a response to these requirements all geographical locations in England have developed multi-agency policies, procedures and practice guidelines for the protection of vulnerable adults. Many of these are available online through local authority websites; others will be available in libraries or through the local authority offices.

ACTIVITY 6.4

Locate a copy of the local policy and procedures for the area which you are living and/or working. Read through the document and answer the following questions:

- *Does the document define key terms? If so, are these a reflection of the definitions in the* No Secrets *document?*

- *Does the document provide a procedural process? If so, does the procedure address each area as outlined in the* No Secrets *document?*

If you are able to obtain two different local policies and procedures you could compare two different approaches. You could work with another student to make this comparison.

The Department of Health would anticipate that the document or documents that you have examined are likely to reflect quite accurately both the definitions and the procedures as stated in their guidance, *No Secrets* (DoH, 2000a). In June 2002, six months after the implementation of the requirements of *No Secrets*, the Centre for Policy on Ageing (Sumner, 2002) was commissioned by the Department of Health to undertake an analysis of local codes of practice for the protection of vulnerable adults. The research focused on: strategies and plans; procedures and protocols; guidance and information. The research report lists 23 key findings separated into areas related to: high-level strategic commitments; detailed strategy programme; key elements of good practice guidance; accessibility and supplementary documentation; and general performance levels. We have extracted a few of the key findings of the research most relevant to the discussion in this section of the chapter in the box below.

RESEARCH SUMMARY

Findings from an analysis of local codes of practice

- *The vast majority of the codes (80 per cent) engaged in significant consultation with local partners.*

- *89 per cent of the codes made cross-agency role allocation and accountabilities clear and explicit.*

- *94 per cent of the codes provided detailed and illustrative 'triggers' to guide staff as to when to intervene in support of an 'abused' adult and when to involve colleagues.*

- *84 per cent of the codes incorporated guidance around working with individuals who are unable to make their own decisions for various reasons, with sections offering guidance on consent, capacity and best interests.*

- *The definitions of abuse detailed in* No Secrets *had been adopted in 82 per cent of the codes.*

Among the conclusions, the research notes that 'a great deal of effort had been put into ensuring detailed operational procedures and practice guidance for staff is available' *but that more work was needed on the requirements in Section 7 of* No Secrets *in relation to the dissemination of information, engaging the public and spreading awareness.*

Extracted from Sumner (2002)

The requirements of *No Secrets* and the resultant local policies and procedures are, however, by no means the only legal context within which social work practice in respect of the protection of vulnerable older people takes place. It is not possible within this book to provide in-depth information about all of the pieces of law, government circulars, codes of practice and policies that are potentially relevant. Therefore we have identified seven national documents that we consider to be significant in terms of social work practice, vulnerability and abuse of older people. In the remainder of this section we briefly outline why these documents are important to social work practice with vulnerable older people. The documents are presented in chronological order. You will find further information about the legal and political context of work with older people in Chapter 3 of this book and in the additional sources detailed at the end of Chapter 3 and this chapter. Additionally the following website addresses will provide you with access and links to information about a large range of legislation:

- www.legislation.hmso.gov.uk/acts/acts

- www.else.org.uk/socialcareresource/legislation

National Health Service and Community Care Act 1990

This key piece of legislation was implemented nationally in 1993. It transformed the system for Community Care in England and resulted in the reform of policies, procedures and organisational structures at a local level. This legislation was supported by practice guidance that detailed procedures necessary to implement the requirements of the act (DoH, 1990a, 1991).

Within this legislation and subsequent guidance the social work processes of assessment, care planning, intervention, monitoring and review are detailed. For example, section 47(1) of the Act sets out the duty to assess need. The act and underpinning guidance describe needs-led assessment with service user involvement in the process. However, Pritchard (2001) suggests that assessments may still focus on material resources, omitting some of the more complex needs that would be particularly essential in situations of potential abuse.

Human Rights Act 1998

The Human Rights Act, which came into force in 2000, applies to all public bodies and requires them to operate in accordance with the European Convention on Human Rights (1950). The Act enables the possibility of challenge on the basis that something (usually an action, decision, policy or procedure) is or was incompatible with human rights. The main areas of the Act that could be considered relevant to social work practice with vulnerable older people are as follows:

Article 2 – the right to life

Article 3 – the right not to be subjected to torture or degrading treatment or punishment

Article 5 – the right to liberty and security of person

Article 8 – the right to respect for private and family life, home and correspondence.

Action for Justice (Home Office, 1999)

Action for Justice followed a Home Office report *Speaking up for Justice* (1998). It is embedded in the Youth Justice and Criminal Evidence Act 1999. This legislation acknowledges the difficulties faced by vulnerable people who are victims and/or witnesses. It attempts to address some of these difficulties with a variety of measures, such as evidence being given in private (section 25), live links enabling the witness to give evidence away from the court (section 24), screens to be made available to protect the witness (section 23) and any other special measures that will help the person to maximise the quality of their evidence. Social work practitioners should use the facilities made available by this legislation to assist and support vulnerable or intimidated older people to provide evidence.

Care Standards Act 2000

In summary, the Care Standards Act reforms the regulatory system for care services in England. It also established new standards in social care work and in the education and training of social workers. The Act is separated into nine parts with Parts I, II and VII being most pertinent to the subject of this chapter.

Part I established a new, independent regulatory body for care services, the National Care Standards Commission (NCSC). The NCSC has responsibility for the registration and quality monitoring of all registered social care services. Section 23(1) of the Care Standards Act, for example, sets out the national minimum standards for care homes for older people. One of the most relevant standards within this section is Standard 18, which sets as its outcome that 'service users are protected from abuse'. This standard is broken down into six requirements, the first of which is given below to show you an example of how the Care Standards Act sets out to protect older people from abuse.

> *18.1 The registered person ensures that service users are safeguarded from physical, financial or material, psychological or sexual abuse, neglect, discriminatory abuse or self-harm, inhuman or degrading treatment, through deliberate intent, negligence or ignorance, in accordance with written policies.*

Part II makes provision for the regulatory procedures which the NCSC implement. This includes the development of national minimum care standards.

Part VII of the Care Standards Act is noteworthy in terms of the protection of vulnerable people in that it sets out the requirement for a register of people deemed unsuitable to work with vulnerable adults who need care in any setting. Employers of staff working with vulnerable adults will be required to refer to the Protection of Vulnerable Adults (POVA) list at the time of recruitment, as well as referring people to the list should they have reason to believe that the person has caused harm to vulnerable adults.

More information on the proposed operation of the scheme can be found on the Department of Health website **www.doh.gov.uk/vulnerableadults/index.htm**.

National Service Framework for Older People (2001)

The National Service Framework for Older People aims to improve the quality and consistency of services for older people through national standards and service models. The framework is also discussed in Chapters 3 and 7 of this book. Overall it sets out eight standards to ensure 'sustainable long-term change' (page 3). We would suggest that the standards that are most relevant to the protection of vulnerable older people are:

- *Standard 1: Rooting out age discrimination* – this standard aims to remove discrimination on the grounds of age. For example, it tackles discriminatory practices of inequality of access to services.

- *Standard 2: Person centred care* – this standard is covered in more detail in Chapter 7 of this book. The standard requires services to 'respect dignity and privacy' and 'recognise individual differences and specific needs including cultural and religious difference' (page 23).

- *Standard 8: The promotion of health and active life in older age* – this standard aims to 'extend the healthy life expectancy of older people' (page 107). This is to be achieved, for example, through the development of health promotion and disease prevention programmes in partnership with communities.

Draft Mental Capacity Bill (2003)

At the time of writing, this bill remains in draft form and is yet to pass through the various stages of the legislative process. However, this could result in an important piece of legislation which may assist professionals with the complex issues of definition and criteria of mental capacity. Additionally the bill proposes a new Court of Protection with extended powers to deal with all decisions for adults who cannot decide for themselves and a new appointment of Public Guardian who would oversee many of the processes outlined in the bill. For more information about the Mental Capacity Bill, access **www.lcd.gov.uk/family/mi/** – this is the Mental Capacity Division of the Department for Constitutional Affairs.

Additionally, in respect of issues related to mental capacity, there are common law concepts. Declaratory relief is a common law concept in that it is not enshrined in statutory law. However, it is a mechanism by which public bodies or individuals can take disputes to the High Court so that particular courses of action that are deemed to be in the best interests of the individual concerned are declared lawful.

In addition to the seven documents outlined above, there are other legal routes that may protect older people in particular circumstance, for example: Guardianship, Court of Protection, Appointeeship, Power of Attorney, Enduring Power of Attorney and Receivership. It is not possible to examine each of these processes here but you can look into them through your further reading, as recommended at the end of this chapter (Johns and Sedgwick, 1999).

The documents outlined above have been highlighted in this text as they are significant in providing the specific legislative and policy context for social workers working with vulnerable older people. Some of these laws and policies could be seen as *preventative*, while others cover issues of *protection*. This brings us back to the ethical debate between protection and vulnerability on the one hand and autonomy and empowerment on the other that we first raised in the earlier section in this chapter that looked at terminology. We shall return to this debate later in the chapter.

It is also vital that practitioners remain mindful of the fact that older people are subject to and can utilise all the current laws and policies of the country as applicable. In other words, the laws related to common assault, theft or equal opportunities might also be relevant and helpful in situations of suspected abuse.

As stated previously, this chapter does not aim to provide detailed information about all of the pieces of law, government circulars, codes of practice and policies that may be relevant to social work practice with older adults considered to be vulnerable and at risk of or experiencing abuse. For additional information you should refer to Chapter 3 of this book, the references within this text and the recommended reading.

Social work processes and skills

So far in this chapter you have explored some of the vocabulary and concepts to be found when working with vulnerable older people. You have also been introduced to some of the key areas of legislation and policy guidance that set the national context for social work practice in this area. With these important underpinning themes in your mind, in this section you will read about the skills and processes of social work practice with older people who are at risk of or who are experiencing abuse. This part of the chapter is organised into sections that broadly correspond with Section 6 of the *No Secrets* document. You may find it useful to have a copy of this document with you to refer to as you work through this part of the chapter.

> *The starting point for dealing successfully with circumstances giving ground for anxiety and allegations of the abuse of vulnerable adults must be that agencies have an organisational framework within which all concerned at the operational level understand the inter-agency policies and procedures, know their own role and have access to comprehensive guidance.*
>
> *The first priority should always be to ensure the safety and protection of vulnerable adults. (DoH, 2000a: 26)*
>
> *Social care workers must:*
>
> - *Protect the rights and promote the interests of service users and carers*
>
> - *Promote the independence of service users whilst protecting them as far as possible from danger or harm*
>
> - *Respect the rights of service users whilst seeking to ensure that their behaviour does not harm themselves or other people.*
>
> (GSCC, 2002)

These two quotations from *No Secrets* and the selected standards of conduct from the General Social Care Council (GSCC) form an important basis for any social worker working with vulnerable adults. Figure 6.1 and the following discussion in this section detail the skills and processes of social work practice where abuse of an older adult is suspected or alleged. You will notice that the information provided in this section is necessarily general. This is because any work of this nature must be informed by local policies, procedures and agreements, with each social work practitioner being responsible for making themselves aware of the relevant documents and requirements.

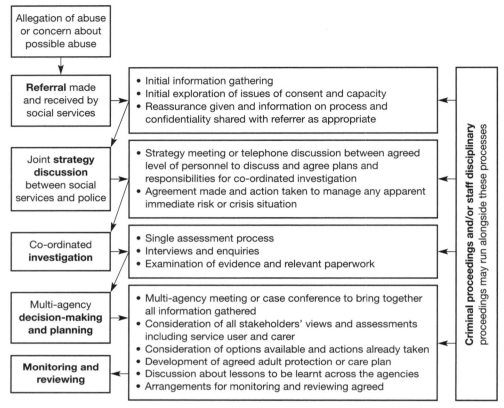

Figure 6.1 Processes of social work practice with older people who are at risk of or who are experiencing abuse

Referral

Information regarding a situation of suspected abuse may arise through a range of sources, but however this occurs you must be mindful that the first priority should be to ensure the safety and protection of the vulnerable adult. At this stage it is very important that as much detailed and clear information is gathered and recorded as is feasible so that decision-making is assisted. Information should include: details about the vulnerable adult, including their situation, care needs and any services currently received; details of the alleged abuse or incident; details about the alleged abuser if known; details about the person making the referral and any immediate action that has been taken. There will usually be specific paperwork and/or software systems used to record this information which must be full, accurate and legible, with fact clearly separated from opinions or judgments.

It is usual for local procedures to require the practitioner who first receives this information to have an early discussion with the police. This will enable joint decision-making and planning, including a decision about whether it is likely that a criminal offence has been committed.

This point of decision-making and planning may also require an early judgment about risk and a possible response to a crisis situation. The police will also want to ensure that any possible forensic evidence is not lost or contaminated for future criminal proceedings. The practitioner receiving the information will also need to consider, at this stage, issues of consent and confidentiality.

ACTIVITY **6.5**

Read the case study below. Imagine that you are the social worker who receives this telephone call. What questions would you ask Katrina's husband?

Katrina is 72 years of age. She was severely injured in a road traffic accident five years ago and following initial hospitalisation has lived in a care establishment with other disabled adults. Katrina has multiple physical difficulties including considerable difficulties with speech. However, she is mentally fully aware and able. Katrina's husband visits his wife daily and is very involved in delivering all of Katrina's care needs. Katrina's husband is the only person who has developed a clear understanding of everything Katrina says, and they communicate with ease. After one of his visits, Katrina's husband telephones social services and states that his wife has informed him that one of the male care staff has touched her between her legs. Katrina is very upset and frightened. The husband is very angry and upset, he wants immediate action to be taken.

You will appreciate that it is not straightforward for the social worker receiving such a call to ask a range of what might be deemed as unnecessary questions. You would need to ascertain information about Katrina, her abilities and her care in the establishment. It may be that the social services agency are already involved in the provision of Katrina's care and therefore some details will already be held. However, certain key facts will be needed in order to access information already held. You should also ask whether she is aware that he is making the telephone call – it is important to know whether she has given consent for this action to be taken. It would also be important to talk to her husband about who she alleges is the abuser, for example does he know the name of the worker and is this alleged to have happened more than once? You would need factual information about Katrina's husband, such as his full name and contact details. Finally and most importantly, you will recall that the first priority should always be to ensure the safety and protection of vulnerable adults, so you will need to know whether any immediate action has been taken. Has the allegation been reported to the manager of the establishment and, if so, is the alleged abuser still in contact with residents? You would also need to provide Katrina's husband with reassurance and information. He will need to know what actions you would plan to take immediately, how his wife will be protected and when he will next be contacted.

All of this information will need to be recorded sensitively, in the appropriate format, in preparation for further discussions, planning and reporting. It would be usual for social workers to discuss such referrals with their supervisor or line manager. Additionally, the social worker may want to consider, at each stage of the process, whether they need to seek legal advice through their agency.

Many local procedures stipulate that joint strategy discussions or meetings should be held to undertake the formal planning and decision-making prior to an investigation being embarked upon. Strategy meetings will facilitate joint working through information sharing, agreement on the proposed plan for the investigation and joint task allocation. The information gathered from the referral stage will be vital to inform the strategy discussion.

Investigation

An investigation should establish and record the facts about the circumstances that have been reported. This should enable a decision about whether abuse has taken place, which will ensure that the vulnerable person is supported, empowered and protected and that appropriate action is taken in respect of any perpetrator. Finally, the investigation should identify whether there are any lessons to be learnt for the professionals and their organisations for the future.

This stage will require a number of tasks to be undertaken. The tasks and responsibilities should be planned following receipt of the referral so that a co-ordinated approach to joint investigation and assessment, where appropriate, is implemented. A co-ordinated approach that incorporates proper information sharing will reduce the possibility of distressing repeat interviews. One of the first tasks is likely to be to undertake a holistic and comprehensive assessment with the older person. In Chapter 7 of this book you will read about the *single assessment process*, which is a requirement of the National Service Framework for Older People (DoH, 2001a) Standard 2 and means that at a local level agencies, teams, individual practitioners, users and carers will work together to gather and share information and decisions in respect of the care services for an individual. The *single assessment process* would be implemented as part of the vulnerable adult investigation.

The starting point for the assessment would be to gain the older person's consent to the gathering of information and this will require an assessment of the mental capacity of the vulnerable adult to provide that consent. As part of this assessment, an immediate and longer-term assessment of risk would be undertaken. This would include consideration of the risks that may be posed to the professionals working in the situation. Additionally, the assessment should include attention to whether there is any need for medical intervention, if this has not already taken place.

As with all aspects of social work with vulnerable older people who may experience abuse, the assessment phase will be sensitive and potentially complex. The social worker will need specific skills and knowledge to facilitate effective communication with the older adult. The older person's communication skills may be hampered by the possible emotional and physical trauma of the events they have experienced. English may not be their first language and they may have sensory or psychological needs that should be taken into account and support with communication offered, if appropriate. Parker and Bradley (2003) set out good assessment skills and ways in which social workers can enable service-users to influence and participate in the assessment process, as they examine different models and types of assessment.

The investigation may also require a range of other involved people to be interviewed; this may be undertaken jointly or by certain professionals alone, according to the agreements made at the planning stage. Furthermore, various documentation or other evidence may come under scrutiny at this stage. Where necessary, the police would carry out a criminal investigation at the same time as the adult abuse investigation is progressing.

Record-keeping

Section 6 of the *No Secrets* document states that 'whenever a complaint or allegation of abuse is made all agencies should keep clear and accurate records' (DoH, 2000a: 30). In the discussion above we have emphasised the importance of full, accurate and legible recording with facts clearly separated from opinions or judgments. Furthermore when recording information about individuals, either in written format or on a computer system, you must ensure that the principles of the Data Protection Act 1998 are adhered to, including consideration that their own file and computer records are available to the service user.

Each agency should have its own procedures and requirements in terms of recording and reporting. These should cover individual case file recording, any requirements to input data onto software systems, reporting processes and the ways in which data will be collated for monitoring and statistical purposes across a wider area.

Planning and decision-making

As with each stage of this process, this should be a multi-agency, multi-professional discussion and decision-making forum. Again, local policies and procedures will determine the practicalities of how this process is undertaken, but as we have seen, the first and main objective of this planning process will be to ensure the safety of vulnerable adults.

The information gathered through the assessment and investigation phase will inform the planning. One of the essential starting points for such a discussion will be reflections on the investigation, in particular drawing out the wishes and feelings of the vulnerable older person. The balance between the person's right to self-determination and the risk to themselves and others may have to be evaluated. We return to the issues of self-determination and empowerment in the next section of this chapter. However, it is important to state here that where a criminal offence may have been committed, this would supersede the individual's rights to autonomy (Hughes, 2001).

The social worker involved in the planning and decision-making of any vulnerable adult situation will need to employ a range of skills and knowledge. Skills of negotiation, communication, joint working and problem-solving will all be essential. The outcome of this stage of the process would be the development of an adult protection plan; this document may be given other names such as a care plan. Arrangements and responsibilities for service provision, monitoring and reviewing of the plan should also be agreed.

Staff discipline and criminal proceedings

As you have seen, abuse may be carried out by a wide range of people; however, when the alleged perpetrator is a member of staff, then additional policies and procedures will be relevant and should be implemented, in particular employment laws and policies including internal disciplinary procedures, professional codes of conduct, professional regulation and registration. Furthermore, it may be another member of staff who is making the allegation, in which case, *whistle-blowing* procedures would be followed in order to protect all of those involved.

Following the fundamental aim to ensure the safety and protection of vulnerable adults, the alleged abuser may be suspended from duties during the period of investigation until a decision is made. Circumstances where a care worker has been accused of abuse and/or bad practice will always be particularly sensitive and traumatic for everyone involved. It is imperative, though, that however difficult it may be, agreed procedures and protocols are followed to ensure the protection and rights of all those involved are ensured.

Vulnerable adults who abuse

You should also consider the specific social work skills and practices that will be necessary where another vulnerable adult is the alleged abuser. The professionals involved should look at whether, in terms of good practice and impartiality, this person should be allocated separate workers, including a different social worker and possibly an advocate. Again, everyone involved will need to consider whether any immediate actions are necessary while an investigation is carried out to ensure the safety and protection of all vulnerable people that this person may have contact with. The alleged abuser should have their needs assessed as part of the investigative process in the same ways as described previously, including risk assessment and assessment of capacity.

Throughout all of these processes, when working with vulnerable older people and their carers you will need to use a range of skills. These will include actively listening and engaging appropriately with the life experiences and perceptions of the service user, and understanding accurately their viewpoint and overcoming all prejudices and assumptions to respond appropriately to such complex personal and interpersonal situations. As a social worker you should continually reflect upon your practices with older adults and make effective use of supervision, support and further learning opportunities to develop the necessary skills.

User perspective

In this chapter so far you have looked at a range of issues that have been largely about processes and structures. Earlier in this chapter we referred to the importance of listening to and understanding the service user experience and ensuring their full participation in the processes. In this section we shall expand upon those concepts and encourage you to consider what this means for social work practice.

The social work subject benchmark statement 3.1.4 Values and ethics states that 'the moral concepts of rights, responsibility, freedom, authority and power [are] inherent in the practice of social workers as moral and statutory agents'. All of these notions can be located in any discussion about work with vulnerable older people who are or may be experiencing abusive situations. These emotive and complex moral concepts are most likely to be debated where the issues of individual rights, collective rights and risks are raised. The social work principles of enabling self-determination can be challenged where the person makes choices that, in the judgment of professionals and/or informal carers, leave them or others at risk.

The social worker and their colleagues in the multi-professional team will be able to bring highly developed skills and a wide range of knowledge to their work with individual vulnerable people. However, the social worker should always consider, in discussion with the service-user, whether the services of an independent advocate or the assistance of a chosen supporter would enable the user to take more control of their situation. In addition there are a number of networks and user groups that may provide valuable information and support to service users and their carers, for example Action on Elder Abuse (**www.elderabuse.org**) and the International Network for the Prevention of Elder Abuse (**www.inpea.net/**).

Another facet to this debate must be the consideration of the individual's capacity to make decisions at this level. We have discussed this earlier and in other chapters of this book and looked at the legal and policy framework around capacity issues.

> *The vulnerable adult's capacity is the key to action since if someone has 'capacity' and declines assistance this limits the help that he or she may be given. It will not, however, limit the action that may be required to protect others who are at risk of harm. In order to make sound decisions, the vulnerable adult's emotional, physical, intellectual and mental capacity in relation to self-determination and consent and any intimidation, misuse of authority or undue influence will have to be assessed. (DoH, 2000a: 31)*

Preston-Shoot (in Bytheway et al., 2002) acknowledges the complexity of this work and the dilemmas faced when making necessary professional judgments and decisions. He distinguishes between 'negative freedom (self-determination as a right)' and 'positive freedom (intervention to enable individuals to become more self-determining)' (page 196). Furthermore he introduces the concepts of 'positive obligation to provide' good and a 'negative obligation to cause no harm' (page 202). This results in a compelling and potentially helpful argument, in that he suggests that the overarching purpose of professional involvement should be to promote self-determination and autonomy. Working with the main objective of empowerment social workers will enable older people to reduce their vulnerability and develop strength, power and autonomy. In this way, protection of older people, which we have argued is the first priority, will be either unnecessary as older people become less vulnerable or they will be empowered to protect themselves.

C H A P T E R S U M M A R Y

In this chapter we have taken a critical approach to defining and understanding vulnerability, abuse, risks and rights regarding social work practice with older people.

After studying a brief outline of the historical context of vulnerability and abuse, you examined some of the terms that are used to describe abusive situations and particular types of abuse, including a consideration of how these terms have adapted and changed over time. You also examined the national policy document on Protection for Vulnerable Adults, *No Secrets: Guidance on developing and implementing multi-agency policies and procedures to protect vulnerable adults from abuse* (DoH, 2000a) and other key documents that provide the legal and political context to social work practice in this area.

This chapter has also looked at the social work practice, processes and skills involved in the identification, investigation and prevention of abuse. In the final section your thoughts on the user perspective were developed, with particular attention to the professional dilemmas that result from the debate between autonomy and protection.

In the chapter we have given prominence to two key areas: working together across disciplines and agencies with inter-agency co-ordination, sharing of information and joint decision-making; and the importance of the user perspective and how the promotion of self-determination and empowerment can assist in developing good practice in respect of social work with vulnerable older people.

You have seen in this chapter how social work practice in situations of alleged abuse can be complex and challenging. In order to develop professionally you should continually reflect upon your practice and your personal professional development. You should take advantage of opportunities to learn through structured supervision and from research and contemporary writing. As a social worker, you are accountable for the quality of your work and must take responsibility for maintaining and improving your knowledge and skills (GSCC, 2002).

Johns, R. and Sedgwick, A. (1999) *Law for Social Work Practice: Working with Vulnerable Adults.* Basingstoke: Palgrave Macmillan.
Although this book was published prior to the publication of *No Secrets* (DoH, 2000a), it provides an accessible text that covers the relevant legislation. Through the use of a case study approach coupled with clear headings, this is a helpful and easily used book.

Bennett, G., Kingston, P. and Penhale, B. (1997) *Dimensions of Elder Abuse. Perspectives for Practitioners.* Basingstoke: Macmillan.
Taking an interdisciplinary approach from a range of perspectives, this book is very useful as it considers practice situations and looks at ways in which practitioners can work towards prevention.

Pritchard, J. (ed.) (2001) *Good Practice with Vulnerable Adults.* London: Jessica Kingsley.
This edited book has 14 chapters that address contemporary practice issues in respect of social work practice with vulnerable adults. It includes perspectives from across a range of disciplines, thus promoting good multi-agency practice.

www.elderabuse.org.uk – Action on Elder Abuse
This is a useful website that not only provides information about research and social policy, but also lists training opportunities and has a range of relevant linked sites.

Chapter 7
Partnership and participation

This chapter will help you to begin to meet the following National Occupational Standards:

Key Role 1: Prepare for and work with individuals, families, carers, groups and communities to assess their needs and circumstances

- Work with individuals, families, carers, groups and communities to help them make informed decisions
- Assess needs and options to recommend a course of action

Key Role 2: Plan, carry out, review and evaluate social work practice with individuals, families, carers, groups, communities and other professionals

- Interact with individuals, families, carers, groups and communities to achieve change and development and to improve life opportunities
- Support the development of networks to meet assessed needs and planned outcomes

Key Role 5: Manage and be accountable with supervision and support for your own social work practice within your organisation

- Work within multi-disciplinary and multi-organisational teams, networks and systems

It will also introduce you to the following academic standards as set out in the social work subject benchmark statement:

3.1.1 Social work services and service users

- The relationship between agency policies, legal requirements and professional boundaries in shaping the nature of services provided in inter-disciplinary contexts and the issues associated with working across professional boundaries and within different disciplinary groups

3.1.2 The service delivery context

- The significance of interrelationships with other social services, especially education, housing, health, income maintenance and criminal justice

3.1.5 The nature of social work practice

- The factors and processes that facilitate effective inter-disciplinary, inter-professional and inter-agency collaboration and partnership

The subject skills highlighted to demonstrate this knowledge in practice include:

3.2.3 Communication skills

- Listen actively to others, engage appropriately with the life experiences of service-users, understand accurately their viewpoint and overcome personal prejudices to respond appropriately to a range of complex personal and interpersonal situations

3.2.4 Skills in working with others

- Involve users of social work services in ways that increase their resources, capacity and power to influence factors affecting their lives
- Consult actively with others, including service users, who hold relevant information or expertise
- Act co-operatively with others, liaising and negotiating across differences such as organisational and professional boundaries and differences of identity or language
- Develop effective helping relationships and partnerships with other individuals, groups and organisations that facilitate change

5.2.1 Knowledge and understanding

- Ability to use this knowledge and understanding in work within specific practice contexts

Introduction

This chapter will consider the knowledge and skills required to develop social work practice with older people that ensures the meaningful participation of all stakeholders. Taking the National Service Framework for Older People (NSF), in particular Standard 2: Single assessment process (SAP), as an example, this chapter will explore the concepts of partnership and participation in practice. You will be reminded of the legal and political context of social work practice with older people through making the links to Chapter 3. You will also learn about some of the historical context to the drives towards partnership working.

The chapter is structured to assist you to explore issues of partnership and participation at different levels. After considering a range of terms related to partnership working, the first section of the chapter will reintroduce the single assessment process. You will then consider the implications for working together at a structural and strategic level. In the next section of the chapter you will explore work within multi-disciplinary teams, networks and systems and the skills required to develop and maintain effective professional working relationships. You will consider the relationship between agency policies, legal requirements and professional boundaries in shaping the nature of services provided in inter-disciplinary contexts and the issues associated with working across professional boundaries.

Throughout the chapter you will learn about the strengths and value of an approach that encompasses a range of professional perspectives but is integrated through an explicit and visible focus on the individual older person at its centre. So in the final section you will look at how older people who use social work services can be enabled to participate in assessment and service provision in ways that will increase their resources, capacity and power to influence factors that affect their lives. In this section you will also explore partnership working with families and informal carers of older people. You will examine how social work practice can support the maintenance and development of networks to meet the needs and wishes of older people.

Terminology and historical context

In Chapter 3 of this book, you were introduced to the National Service Framework for Older People (DoH, 2001a). In his introduction in the document, Alan Milburn, the then Secretary of State for Health, describes the framework as '... the first ever comprehensive strategy to ensure fair, high quality, integrated health and social care services for older people' (page i). Milburn also explains how older people and their carers were consulted in the development of the framework. It is these two threads of partnership and participation that we will be examining in this chapter: partnership across agencies and professionals; partnership with and participation of older people and their carers.

The National Service Framework for older people has considerable potential consequences for the future of joint working and 'the lead role of social services in community care for older people' (Means et al., 2003: 125) – Standard 2 of the NSF requires the implementation of a single assessment process and means that at a local level agencies, teams and individual practitioners will need to work together and share information and decisions in respect of the care services for older people. Thus this process provides a useful example through which to explore issues of partnership and participation at all levels.

Within this book we have developed a theme of 'continuity and change'. The debates and concepts within this chapter can also been seen to have a historical context while also being subject to change. The notion of working together is not new, with debates about the divisions between health and social care having frustrated practitioners for many years.

In the early 1970s, largely as a result of the National Health Service Act 1973, what appeared as clear divisions between health and social care services were implemented. Local authority social services or welfare departments and district health authorities took up specific areas of responsibility. Yet even with the apparently clear separation of roles, there was much debate about the appropriateness of the different forms of care for certain individuals (Means et al., 2003). The 1980s saw the Audit Commission report *Making a Reality of Community Care* (Audit Commission, 1986) reinforce concerns about the divide between organisations with the Department of Health White Paper *Caring for People: Community Care in the Next Decade and Beyond* (DoH, 1989) and the subsequent NHS and Community Care Act 1990 redefining the roles and relationships between health, social services, voluntary and private care services. It could be argued, though, that the emphasis on market forces at this time, with divisions between commissioners and service providers and complex financial arrangements across agencies, did more to hinder integrated working than to assist working across boundaries. During the 1990s and into the twenty-first century, the concerns about poorly co-ordinated services and the range of innovative attempts to address the concerns show no signs of abating. The Research summary below, demonstrates the continuing concerns that have been articulated over recent years.

RESEARCH BOX

Caring for People: Community Care in the Next Decade and Beyond (1989)

The Government recognises that further efforts are needed to improve co-ordination between health and social services ...

Successful collaboration requires a clear, mutual understanding of each agency's responsibilities and powers, of who decides what, and of how the money flows. This understanding will also help to clarify how and by whom collaboration should be secured. (DoH, 1989: 49 and 50)

The Coming of Age: Improving care services for older people (1997)

Older people often experience care services that are poorly co-ordinated. All too often health and social services fail to agree their respective responsibilities, resulting in confusion and sometimes delays to discharge from hospital ...

While the need for health and social services to work ever more closely together is widely acknowledged, the practicalities of doing so can be very difficult. (Audit Commission, 1997:17 and 53)

> ## National Service Framework for Older People (2001)
>
> *Assessments are often duplicated with no coherent approach across health and social care services. This problem is exacerbated by the fragmentation of information systems, which may unnecessarily duplicate information held about individuals. (DoH, 2001a: 24)*

Along with the many new initiatives and policy directives, in recent years there have come a whole range of different words that are used to describe different aspects of partnership working.

ACTIVITY 7.1

Look at the list of words given below and think about what they mean to you. How would you explain what these words mean? Write down a definition for each term.

- *Multidisciplinary*

- *Health and social care communities*

- *Joint investment plans*

- *Integrated*

- *Joint commissioning arrangements*

- *Partnership*

- *Collaborative approach*

All of these terms appear within the NSF for Older People, yet only three of them are defined within the Glossary of Terms.

RESEARCH SUMMARY

The National Service Framework for Older People (2001) Annex 1, provides the following definitions:

Health and social care communities	Local health authority, local council, NHS Trusts, primary care groups and trusts and the independent sector.
Joint investment plans	Agreed between health and local authorities, JIPs are detailed three-year rolling plans for investment and reshaping of services.
Multidisciplinary	Multidisciplinary refers to when professionals from different disciplines – such as social work, nursing occupational therapy – work together.

(DoH, 1991a)

You may find some of these definitions helpful; however, the Framewor[...] what it means by the other terms you looked at in Activity 7.1:

- integrated
- joint commissioning arrangements
- partnership
- collaborative approach.

Additionally you will come across other related phrases, such as:

- multi-agency
- inter-professional
- inter-agency
- joint working
- whole system approach.

Agreeing clear definitions for each of these terms is not straightforward. A number of the words have meanings which could overlap, while others have disputed or debated meanings. However, the definitions given here aim to provide you with a broad understanding of the concept conveyed by each term:

Integrated	Combined or united into a single entity, system or organisation.
Joint commissioning arrangements	Procedures and agreements whereby two or more agencies purchase and pay for certain services.
Partnership	A relationship built upon mutual agreement, an alliance, an affiliation.
Collaborative approach	Taking a co-operative attitude, joining and sharing knowledge and skills.
Multi-agency	More than one agency.
Inter-professional	Joint working between separate but related professionals, e.g. district nurses, social workers, occupational therapists.
Inter-agency	Within and between agencies.
Joint working	Very similar to 'collaborative working' – co-operative working together.
Whole system approach	An approach to working that ensures that all the interdependent parts of a complex system work to deliver the benefits of the combined structure ('the sum of the parts being greater than the individual parts').

These concepts of integration and joint working operate at different levels within society: at the macro or structural level where strategy, planning and resource issues are consid-

gency, the professional and the teams in which they work
nicro or individual level, where the care needs and services
are agreed and provided for. Taking the single assessment
le in the following sections of this chapter, you will learn
tion at each of these levels.

t process and joint working

ce Framework for Older People encompasses the require-
professionals work together at all levels. As discussed in Chapter
3, a key element of Standard 2 is the *single assessment process (SAP)*.

RESEARCH SUMMARY

National Service Framework for Older People (DoH 2001) Standard 2: Person-centred care

Aim

To ensure that older people are treated as individuals and receive appropriate and timely packages of care which meet their needs as individuals, regardless of health and social services boundaries.

Standard

NHS and social care services treat older people as individuals and enable them to make choices about their own care. This is achieved through the single assessment process, integrated commissioning arrangements and integrated provision of services, including community equipment and continence services.

(DoH, 2001a: 23)

In its *Guidance for Local Implementation*, the Department of Health states that the SAP should 'ensure that the scale and depth of assessment is kept in proportion to older people's needs, agencies do not duplicate each others' assessments, and professionals contribute to assessments in the most effective way' (DoH, 2002a: 1). Thus through the implementation of the single assessment process the government aims to improve the coherence of assessments, making them comprehensive, reducing duplication and ensuring that thorough assessments lead to co-ordinated service provision. 'Assessment is part of a continual process which links with planning, intervening and reviewing ...' (Parker and Bradley, 2003: 8).

Partnership and participation at a strategic level

In this section we shall consider partnership working in agencies at the level where strategy, planning and resource issues are considered. You will begin by considering some of the difficulties that face the two key agencies of health and social care when they work together at a strategic level. You will also look at the possible motives for working together at this level and some of the incentives or strategies that have been put forward to drive joint working. Through the discussion you will be alerted to how the single assessment process provides a vivid illustration of many of these factors.

The NSF sets out that the SAP should be implemented by April 2004 in local areas. Agencies were required to develop project plans based upon the 12 steps of implementation laid out by the Department of Health in the *Guidance for Local Implementation*. These steps are given below:

1. Agree purpose and outcomes

2. Agree shared values

3. Agree terminology

4. Map care processes

5. Estimate the types and number of older people needing assessment

6. Agree the stages of assessment and care management

7. Agree the link between medical diagnosis and assessment

8. Agree the domains and sub-domains of assessment

9. Agree assessment approaches, tools and scales

10. Agree joint working arrangements

11. Agree a single assessment summary

12. Implement a joint staff development strategy.

(DoH, 2002a)

Each of these steps requires joint working and partnership at the agency level. However, the decisions made and agreements forged through this strategic planning towards the implementation of the SAP will directly influence the assessment process that each older person in that local area experiences.

ACTIVITY 7.2

Read through the phases or steps of implementation above. What are the common themes that emerge from these requirements?

You will remember that the guidance is directed at staff within a range of agencies that are working to implement the SAP. This will include GP surgeries, a range of community and acute health services, primary care trusts, local authority social services, voluntary sector representatives and service user and carer groups. One of the starkest commonalities that emerge from the 12 steps of implementation is the need for *agreement* and, by implication, mutual trust. This may seem straightforward on the face of it, but if you consider the complexities of geographical boundaries, internal agency changes, issues of funding, the range of different roles and responsibilities and different professional cultures and jargon, this is anything but straightforward.

In an attempt to overcome these difficulties, the first two steps require the professionals to *agree purpose and outcomes* and to *agree shared values*. In this way, it is felt that the foundations of shared principles, including principles about how disagreements will be managed (Malin et al., 1999; Means et al., 2003), become set and the way is cleared for open and honest discussion.

This, however, may simplify what is a multi-faceted and complex issue. Lewis (2002) suggests that the boundary between health and social care for older people can be seen to have three main dimensions which are entwined.

RESEARCH SUMMARY

The health/social care boundary has three main dimensions:

Financial
Each agency is differently funded, with health care being provided free and social care being charged for. Resources across both agencies are limited and expenditure has to be prioritised.

Administrative
Since the 1948 National Assistance Act, there have been continuous changes to each agency's responsibilities and inconsistent definitions of health care and social care.

Professional rivalries
There have been long-standing differences in the ways in which health and social care professionals work, the models they use and their professional identity.

(Lewis, 2002)

The implementation of the single assessment process will challenge all the relevant agencies to address issues within these three dimensions. Financially there has been no specific funding made available to agencies to assist with the development work and implementation costs of the SAP, so agreement about sharing of costs will be essential to productive joint working. The single assessment process will also require fundamental agreements about common approaches to assessment, responsibilities and processes, working through the administrative and professional dimensions of the divide between the agencies. Thus before different organisations with potentially different priorities, objectives and values can address each of these *dimensions* there has to be a desire and motive to work together.

Working in partnership at all levels, but particularly at this strategic level, can lead to certain losses or risks for the agency, which need to be balanced against the potential gains. Before we introduce ways in which collaborative working can be fostered, you need to understand what some of the difficulties or barriers to joint working at this level might be.

A useful framework through which to explore issues of partnership working has been developed as the outcome of research undertaken by the Nuffield Centre for Community Care Studies (2000) on behalf of the Joint Future Group of the Scottish Executive. This *Integrated Working Project* research examined a range of case studies and focused on 'the nature of integrated working and in particular the challenges encountered and solutions developed'. One of the outcomes of this work was the identification of *drivers* and *barriers* to well-integrated working. The *drivers* (or 'things that assist integrated working') and *barriers* (or 'things that hinder integrated working') have been organised into a matrix, within which they are grouped into three main areas: *National Policy Frameworks*; *Local Planning Context*; and *Operational Factors*. The first two of these areas are particularly pertinent to the strategic level of decision-making (see Table 7.1). You will read about the third area, *Operational Factors*, later in this chapter.

Table 7.1 Drivers and barriers to well-integrated working

NATIONAL POLICY FRAMEWORKS	
Drivers	**Barriers**
• Comprehensive and integrated	• Piecemeal and contradictory
• Encourage strategic approach	• Promote 'projectitis'
• Legal, financial and guidance frameworks facilitate	• Legal, financial and guidance frameworks inhibit
• Realistic timescales	• Unrealistic timescales/change agenda
• Some non-negotiables	• Anything goes!
• Establish accountability for user focused outcomes	• No national pressure to demonstrate user benefit

LOCAL PLANNING CONTEXT	
Drivers	**Barriers**
• Planning and decision cycles mesh	• Incompatible planning and decision cycles
• All stakeholders involved from the beginning: unions, operational staff, users and carers	• Partial/tokenistic involvement of stakeholders
• Joint acceptance of unmet needs	• Not needs led
• Agreed, comprehensive vision, owned at all levels	• Issues seen in isolation, priorities not agreed, based on lowest common denominator
• User outcome driven	• Driven by vested interests
• Evidence based	• A paper strategy
• Runs with 'good enough' plan, 'leap of faith'	• Waits for the perfect plan
• Use of budgets reflects strategic priorities	• 'Spend this money NOW!'
• Some stability	• Constant restructuring
• Shared location	• Dispersed locations
• Small can be good – knowing the people (but no alternatives!)	• Complexity a barrier (but can be an incentive too)
• Builds on existing good working relationships, 'success breeds success'	• No track record of successful collaboration, 'it has never worked here'
• Restricted resources induce innovation – need to share, 'less means more', Dunkirk spirit	• Resources induce complacency – rest on laurels, 'more of the same'
• Pressure to innovate/change to meet need, 'we can't do it alone', 'necessity is the mother of invention'	• No incentives to change 'it won't work here', 'it won't work now'
• Sense of momentum – 'the time is now'	• Baggage of the past

Source: Nuffield Centre for Community Care Studies (2000).

The drivers and barriers shown in Table 7.1 relate to the strategic, planning and policy contexts of joint working. As you can see, they are many and complex. Each organisation or agency needs to appreciate this complexity and work towards putting as many of the drivers in place, as is possible.

Furthermore, if organisations are to be motivated to commit to participating in a joint process they *'need to be persuaded that it is only by this route that organisational objectives can be achieved'* (Means et al., 2003: 114). Means et al. cite the work of Hudson (1987) who proposed a model of three strategies that will assist the development of collaborative working:

- *Co-operative strategies* that are formed through mutual understanding and collaboration.

- *Incentive strategies* which encourage agencies to work together through inducements and reward.

- *Authoritative strategies* whereby agencies are directed and told that they must work together.

(Hudson, 1987, cited in Means et al., 2003: 114)

ACTIVITY **7.3**

Consider the three strategies above. Can you identify where these are relevant in the government's drive to implement the single assessment process?

It is possible to see strands of each of these strategies within recent government initiatives. For example, agencies which are not successful in implementing the single assessment process by the target date of April 2004, or who cannot show significant steps have been made towards having it in place, will be required to adopt a system and process specified for them by the Department of Health. Thus authoritative strategies are being employed as well as an incentive strategy, in that those areas that are successful will not have to comply with an imposed system. However, given the earlier discussion in this chapter about the significance of trust and agreement between agencies, we would question whether such partnership qualities can be engendered through authoritarian and penalising processes (Means et al., 2003).

The National Service Framework for Older People is one of a number of initiatives that the government has introduced in recent years with the aim of removing some of the barriers to integration and providing incentives to encourage agencies to work together. Other significant developments are summarised below. These are also discussed in greater detail in Chapter 3 of this book.

Health Act 1999

Section 31 of this legislation introduced *partnership flexibilities*, which allow the National Health Service and local authorities to pool budgets, agree on a *lead commissioner* and integrate services across the traditional organisational boundaries. In effect, each of these permissions could be described as *incentive and authoritative strategies* as partnership working is not only encouraged but made a duty through them.

Care Trusts

Within the NHS Plan (DoH, 2000d) and then in section 45 of the 2001 Health and Social Care Act the integration of health and social care services through the creation of Care Trusts was introduced. These single legal entities are responsible for local health and social care. Here again, you will recognise an incentive, encouraging and enabling strategy. However, the NHS Plan also made it clear that where agencies 'have failed to establish effective joint partnerships ... the Government will take powers to establish integrated arrangements through the new Care Trust' (DoH, 2000d). So authoritative and directive strategies have also been built in.

Local Government Act 2000 – local strategic partnerships (LSPs)

The Local Government Act 2000 incorporated powers for authorities to work in partnership with agencies in their locality to develop community strategies to reduce social deprivation and enhance social inclusion. LSPs will be responsible for co-ordinating statutory, private and voluntary sector bodies, thereby providing a framework for overseeing local partnership arrangements.

These examples illustrate the administrative and financial strategies that operate at the macro or structural level. You may feel that the examples and concepts that you have read about in this section seem distanced from issues of partnership between teams and individual professionals or from the experience of older people. However, these strategies have a direct bearing upon partnership and participation throughout each level of care service. As you read the rest of this chapter, you will explore issues of partnership working and participation between agencies, teams and professionals and then consider how services work in partnership with older people and their carers.

Partnership and participation at an agency, professional and team level

Having explored partnership working from the structural level where strategy, planning and resource issues are considered, in this section you will consider how agencies, different professionals and teams work together. You will consider the SAP in more detail, as an example of how one area of integrated working, assessment, might impact upon older people using social work services.

In some areas of the country and within some specific service areas, joint teams have been established. The precise configuration, management and service delivery modes of such teams will vary enormously.

CASE STUDY

Community Older Persons Team (Copt), Knowsley, North West of England

Copt is an integrated service approach to meeting the social and health care needs of vulnerable older people. The team was established in 2000 with the aim of providing a single point of access to services for older people. Within the team are occupational therapists, physiotherapists, therapy assistants, district nurse assessors, a pharmacist, a health visitor, home safety advisers, social workers, a podiatrist, a community nurse and administrative staff. The team operates out of the same premises, with common day-to-day protocols, integrated policies and ways of working. The team allocates work through joint referral meetings and accepts assessment decisions and enables commissioning across the disciplines. (Hopkins, 2003: 42–3)

This service provides an example of successful integrated working practices. It appears that within this service, the professionals have negotiated and overcome issues related to working across professional boundaries. Earlier in this chapter we introduced the work of Jane Lewis who described *professional rivalries* and the formation of *professional identity* as one of the main dimensions of the health and social care divide (Lewis, 2002). These notions of *boundaries*, individual *identities* and *rivalries* all invoke images of an inward-looking, narrow approach to professional practice. This impression arises from the fact that different professional groups undertake different education and training, may have different core principles and may work from different perspectives or use different models and theoretical approaches to their practices. All of these differences may result in different underpinning values, ideologies, priorities, use of language and behaviour. However, such differences across disciplines have the effect of providing a uniformity within each discipline and thereby a professional identity that each professional can recognise and feel a part of. Once individual workers adopt the recognised professional identity they may feel threatened or undervalued if their skills, knowledge and the range of tasks they perform are to be shared across other professional disciplines. Within health and social care agencies there is usually a range of explicit and implicit hierarchical structures that also impact upon each practitioner's sense of their identity as a professional and who they relate to within the organisation. This concept of hierarchical status relates to issues of power and equality, which may also be threatened by concepts of joint working, sharing information and accepting the professional judgments and decisions of others.

It is important, therefore, that as professional social workers we recognise not only the value of our own contribution to the multi-disciplinary arena, but the value of the skills and knowledge that other professionals bring. Recognising the interdependence between professionals and agencies is a fundamental starting point for effective joint working. Whether you are working within a multi-disciplinary team, such as the Copt team described above, or you are working within a single agency team, you will need to develop the skills and ability to practise within a range of networks to develop and maintain effective working relationships.

Some of these concepts have also been identified within the Integrated Working Project, introduced earlier in this chapter, which undertook research and identified drivers and barriers to effective integrated working. These were organised into three areas: National Policy Frameworks and Local Planning Context, which you explored earlier, and Operational Factors which you will read about below.

The Nuffield Centre for Community Care Studies further subdivides Operational Factors into seven areas: Relations Between Partners, Organisational Culture, Change Management, Enabling Staff, Professional Behaviour, Attitudes and Outcomes. Table 7.2 outlines examples of the drivers and barriers from each of these sections. You may wish to look at these in more detail by visiting their website **www.gla.ac.uk/centres/nuffield/**.

Table 7.2 Drivers and barriers within Operational Factors

OPERATIONAL FACTORS Relations Between Partners	
Drivers	**Barriers**
• Balance of power	• Power imbalance, strong empires, personal sovereignty
• Informed by knowledge across settings, e.g. through joint posts and well selected managers	• Integrated working depends only on personal links

OPERATIONAL FACTORS Organisational Culture	
Drivers	**Barriers**
• Cross boundary working WITHIN agencies	• Competitive
• It is everybody's agenda including accountants, administrators	• Rigid, high bureaucratic controls, 'everything has to be checked'

OPERATIONAL FACTORS Change Management	
Driver	**Barriers**
• Commitment and flexibility to solve ongoing problems	• Notches up new projects, mainstream services unaffected
• Process driven by individuals with leadership qualities and enthusiasm/managers with knowledge of different settings	• Resources too tight, fully committed to existing buildings/staff/ways of working

OPERATIONAL FACTORS Enabling Staff	
Drivers	**Barriers**
• Collaboration and negotiation valued and part of training	• 'More paperwork! More procedures!', 'What is the purpose of all this?'
• Clarity of purpose transmitted to staff and users	• Unclear responsibilities, conflict

OPERATIONAL FACTORS Professional Behaviour	
Drivers	**Barriers**
• Centred on user need	• Tribal, protectionist, different terms and conditions
• Accept challenges to mindset and learns	• Threatened and restrictive

OPERATIONAL FACTORS Attitudes	
Drivers	**Barriers**
• 'We have nothing to lose', 'we have everything to gain'	• 'Not as interesting as my pet project', 'not a model we recognise', 'doesn't fit our procedures'
• 'I am confident in my skills – though I have more to learn and I respect your skills'	• 'I'm not sure what I know and I'm threatened by what you know', 'this is my turf!'

OPERATIONAL FACTORS Outcomes	
Drivers	**Barriers**
• User focused and defined outcomes	• Outcomes only seen from agency's agenda
• Benefits shared	• Winners and losers

Extracted from Nuffield Centre for Community Care Studies (2000).

e noted earlier when looking at the other areas of integrated working identified through
research, this 'matrix of integrated working' offers an in-depth and detailed look at various approaches that either help or hinder successful integrated working practices.

ACTIVITY 7.4

The Community Older Persons Team (Copt) described earlier in the chapter provides an integrated service approach. Look back at the summary details about this service now. Can you identify any of the drivers or barriers operating in this example?

You only have limited information. However, you know that the Copt team accepts each others' assessment decisions and can arrange and purchase services across the boundaries of the disciplines. It is likely therefore that individual team members work with the attitude that drives integrated working, being 'confident in my skills – though I have more to learn and I respect your skills'. You know too that this service has a clear overarching aim, common protocols and policies. You could then surmise that the drivers of 'clarity of purpose transmitted to staff and users' and 'centred on user need' are also evident.

While the importance of user-led services is apparent throughout the Nuffield Centre for Community Care Studies research, the final section that focuses on *Operational Factors – outcomes* underlines the significance of 'user focused and defined outcomes' as a key driver to effective joint working.

The following case study will be used to explore and illustrate some of these concepts and issues.

CASE STUDY

Shirley Bundle is 68 years old, lives alone and has never been married. Her nearest relative is a cousin who lives ten miles away but visits frequently and telephones almost daily. Miss Bundle lives in a second-floor flat, which she rents privately. She has lived there for ten years. The flat is not well serviced, having only one wall-mounted gas heater and an unreliable electric water heater. She has little contact with her immediate neighbours as they are mostly young families with busy lives of their own. The flat is situated in a small rural village which has an infrequent bus service to the nearest town. Until her retirement three years ago, Miss Bundle worked for 30 years in a local factory doing shift work. She would supplement this income with part-time private cleaning jobs. On leaving the factory, Miss Bundle continued her cleaning jobs; however, over the past six-months she has gradually lost each of these jobs due to her ill-health. This is resulting in some financial problems and she is having difficulties making her rent payments.

Miss Bundle has lived with an arthritic condition for some time. This causes her a lot of pain, particularly in her back (spine) and upper body. About a year ago, her GP diagnosed post-menopausal osteoporosis, which is a degenerative condition. This has resulted in a difficult gait and a stooped posture. Miss Bundle lacks strength in her joints and muscles and finds it hard to stand for more than a few minutes. The extent of her difficulties appears to have increased rapidly recently.

CASE STUDY CONTINUED

Miss Bundle has always described herself as being 'not very bright'. She is able to manage all her own affairs, but is not able to deal with complex concepts or concentrate for any length of time. More recently she has started to repeat things and sometimes fails to respond at all, remaining silent and staring into space.

Miss Bundle is now experiencing increasing difficulties in all areas of her life. She has low self-esteem and low mood at present, has a poor appetite, is hardly sleeping at night and has little motivation to pursue previous leisure and recreational activities. Her GP reports that she has experienced 'periods of depression' for some time and she is prescribed anti-depressant medication.

Following one of her regular visits, Miss Bundle's cousin telephones the GP as she is very concerned about her relative's health and safety in the flat. The GP agrees to call and visit Miss Bundle at home.

ACTIVITY **7.5**

List the different agencies that Miss Bundle may come into contact with.

It is difficult to know exactly which agencies would become involved in this scenario, as this will depend upon her needs and wishes but also on how services are configured in her geographical location and the services available. However, Figure 7.1 represents the potential range of professionals and agencies that may become a part of Miss Bundle's care arrangements.

Completing this activity and looking at Figure 7.1 will help you to appreciate not only the high number of people who may work with one older person, but also how that individual may feel powerless and confused by the amount of different people involved in their care. In Figure 7.1 we have included Miss Bundle's neighbours and relative to demonstrate the full extent of her networks. However, for this section of the chapter we shall focus on those agencies and individuals who are within the formal networks of her care. The case example we are using is not unusual, in that it illustrates the potential need for workers from the voluntary, independent and statutory sector agencies to work together in respect of one older person's needs. Each agency will have policies, procedures, structure, organisation, aims and objectives that are unique to the specific service. Within each agency, too, there could be a number of different professionals involved, each of whom have different training, qualifications, backgrounds, codes of practice and professional identities.

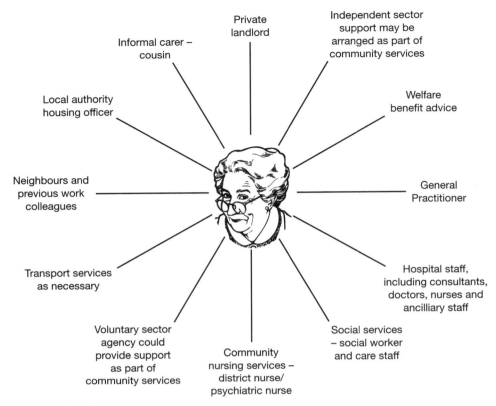

Figure 7.1 *Miss Bundle and professionals*

The potential for confusion, duplication, fragmentation and error is easy to see. It is important, therefore, that you develop not only an appreciation of the possible difficulties inherent in partnership working, but also develop the skills and understanding to over-come these issues in your own practice. In this book, we take the stance that each profession and agency has a significant contribution to make to the whole integrated approach, but that this *whole system approach* will only be effective if it is organised and centred around the older person.

The Audit Commission report Integrated Services for Older People states that:

> Working as a whole system means that services are organised around the user…
>
> • All players recognise their interdependence
>
> • Vision, action, resources and risk are all shared
>
> • Users experience services as seamless

(Audit Commission, 2002)

As the case study illustrates, there is a potential need for a large number of agencies and professionals to work together. Meaningful and effective collaboration requires a range of skills, knowledge and understanding to be exhibited by all of the professionals involved.

You read earlier in this chapter about how the Single Assessment Process requires agencies to *agree purpose and outcomes* and to *agree shared values*. This implies an agreement and acceptance about the diversity of different professions and the value of the different perspectives, skills and knowledge that they can contribute to a complex process. In the same way that we have discussed the value and strengths of each individual older person, so each professional worker, whichever the discipline they represent, should value the opportunities and strengths that working across boundaries can offer. This is another way of acknowledging the truth in the saying 'the whole is greater than the sum of the parts'.

The single assessment process then is one example of an assessment process. It is set to become the only model to be used to assess the holistic needs and circumstances of older people. All other formats or areas of assessment, for example risk assessments, social care assessments, specialist assessments, will fall within the single assessment process.

The government guidance details four types of assessment that fall within the process. These are as follows:

- *Contact assessment* includes the initial collection of basic personal information. It is envisaged that any member of staff from any relevant agency who is appropriately trained could complete this assessment with the older person.

- *Overview assessment* is a more detailed assessment, which collates a more complete outline of the whole older person and their needs. This would include a basic assessment of physical, social and emotional needs as shown by the domains which are discussed below. Following an overview assessment, the need for appropriate, specialist assessments may be identified. Again it is expected that any suitably qualified practitioner from the relevant agencies could commence and, as appropriate, complete this type of assessment.

- *Specialist assessments* take an in-depth examination of one particular aspect of the older person's needs. This assessment would be carried out by the most appropriate professional to assess the specific area of need, as identified through the *overview assessment*. It is likely that many of the pre-existing forms of assessment and assessment tools will fall under this category, for example the district nursing assessment or social work assessment.

- *Comprehensive assessment* would be completed where an individual older person is deemed to have multiple complex needs which require an intensive and multi-faceted plan of care. This assessment will be the culmination of the other types of assessment, which would be brought together into this comprehensive summary.

It is important to understand that these do not constitute *levels* of assessment but are, rather, different forms or types of assessment. It is fundamental to the SAP that each professional will accept and work with each others' completed assessments, across professional disciplines and across agency boundaries. Within these different types of assessment, agencies and professionals need to give consideration to the content of assessments. Within the NSF for Older People, the Department of Health has stated that the overview assessment should include a number of *domains* and *sub-domains*. These are given in the Research box below.

Single assessment process – overview assessment

User's perspective
- Problems and issues in the user's own words
- User's expectations and motivation

Mental health
- Cognition including dementia
- Mental health including depression

Safety
- Abuse or neglect
- Other aspects of personal safety
- Public safety

Clinical background
- History of medical problems
- History of falls
- Medication use

Senses
- Sight
- Hearing
- Communication

Relationships
- Social contacts, relationships and involvement
- Caring arrangements

Disease prevention
- History of blood pressure monitoring
- Nutrition

- Vaccination history
- Drinking and smoking history
- Exercise pattern
- History of cervical and breast screening

Personal care and physical well-being
- Personal hygiene, including washing, bathing, toileting and grooming
- Dressing
- Pain
- Oral health
- Foot-care
- Tissue viability
- Mobility
- Continence
- Sleeping patterns

Immediate environment and resources
- Care of the home
- Accommodation
- Finances
- Access to local facilities and services

(DoH, 2002a: 32–3)

By considering the domains above and their sub-domains you will see how attention to each of these areas should lead to holistic practice, which requires collaboration and information-sharing across professional boundaries.

The practical aspects and working arrangements that reflect effective joint working will vary according to the individual situation. At one end of the continuum, where one professional needs information or advice from another, this may be carried out by a telephone call, e-mail or postal correspondence. At the other end of the continuum, where the skills and knowledge of a range of professionals is necessary, planning meetings, joint assessments and case discussions may be appropriate.

In order to effectively implement the single assessment process social workers will need to 'update their skills and knowledge so that they are able to work effectively with older people, other disciplines and the assessment procedures'. Social workers 'play an important role in contributing to, or co-ordinating, assessment and care planning where a number of agencies are involved' (DoH, 2002b). Therefore the core skills of co-ordination and communication are fundamental to effective working across professional boundaries.

Figure 7.2 represents the many agencies and professionals that may be involved in assessing and meeting the needs of one older person. The complexity of the diagram illustrates the real-life complexity of effectively delivering a co-ordinated, comprehensive range of services. Such services need to be delivered across organisational and professional boundaries using an integrated approach. The SAP is seen as the key mechanism for delivering that approach and ensuring that the older person is central to the process.

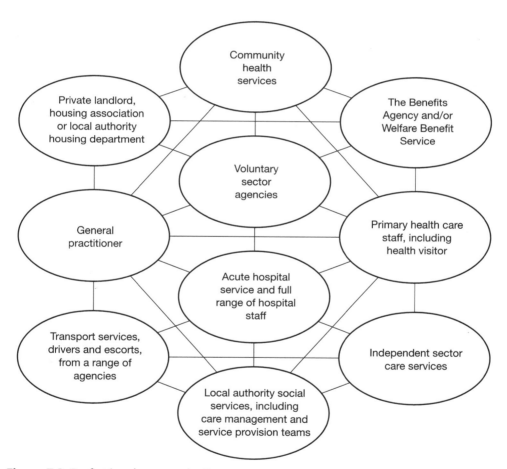

Figure 7.2 Professional communication

ACTIVITY **7.6**

Reread the case study of Miss Shirley Bundle. Think about what might happen next in this scenario. If this was happening before the implementation of the single assessment process, how many assessments might Miss Bundle experience? Which professionals would undertake these assessments? How might this be different if this was happening after the SAP had been implemented?

Prior to the implementation of the SAP, each professional that comes into contact with Miss Bundle will instigate an assessment. Therefore, potentially, her general practitioner, the district nurse, a community psychiatric nurse, the social worker, the housing officer, the hospital admissions team and any other agencies that are requested to provide a service would undertake an assessment. Within their assessments would be a varied range of information including some or all of the following: basic information, general information, specialist information, details relating to risk factors, information about resources (possibly covering financial resources and personal networks) and carers' needs and wishes. It is possible that Miss Bundle could be asked to provide basic details, such as name and date of birth, as many as ten or twelve times throughout this process.

As you have seen, the SAP aims to eradicate duplication, ensuring that assessment and care planning are co-ordinated and effective. Each professional should contribute to the overall assessment in the most effective way, with the scale and depth of the assessment being kept in proportion to the older person's needs. Therefore Miss Bundle should only be asked for core information at the start of the process, with this being shared across professionals as the assessment is progressed. So, while there would still be a number of specialists involved, each with particular knowledge and skills, they would add their specialist assessments to the contact and overview assessments, which in this scenario are likely to have been completed. The single assessment process will ensure that the service user only has to provide core information about her problems once, irrespective of the number of professionals involved.

As you have seen, effective communication is vital even with the implementation of the SAP. For communication to flow efficiently in such complex and changing situations, between organisations and individuals, a range of information technology (IT) systems offers the most straightforward and speedy solution. Communication through this medium can be held back when different agencies or individuals do not have compatible systems. However, when effective systems that connect across the agencies are in use, the possibilities range from shared databases, shared information and performance management systems through to individual e-mailing.

As the different professionals work with individual older people, they will accumulate a range of detailed information. Such information should be maintained and stored so that it can be shared across agencies, with the older person's consent, subject to confidentiality and the requirements and provisions of the Data Protection Act 1998.

Partnership and participation with older people and their carers

Throughout this chapter so far, you have been looking at partnership working from a strategic level and from the perspective of the agencies and professionals. However, the significance of maintaining a focus on the individual older person, i.e. being user-centred, has been shown to be the overarching and underpinning value that will assist agencies and professionals to work towards a common goal. In this part of the chapter you will consider the issues of partnership from the perspective of older people, their families and informal carers. You will explore ways in which older people who use social work services can be enabled to participate in assessment and service provision so as to increase their resources, capacity and power to influence factors that affect their lives. Through your studies of this section of the chapter you will learn how social work practice can support the maintenance and development of networks to meet the needs and wishes of older people. As before, we shall continue to use the single assessment process to illustrate the discussion.

Earlier in this book we have discussed the problematic nature of the social construction of age, stereotyping and making assumptions about older people being one homogenous group of people who experience similar issues and difficulties. Each of us is growing older all of the time and our experiences of all aspects of developing and ageing are different and unique to us as individuals. Therefore as social workers we need to be continually mindful of diversity and the personal, distinctive nature of each individual's development and experiences. In order to appreciate and understand the older person's perspective and the experiences that underpin their views and priorities, social workers must take a biographical or narrative approach (Crawford and Walker, 2003; Gubrium and Holstein, 2003; Richards, 2000).

RESEARCH SUMMARY

Bridging the Divide: Elders and the Assessment Process

Using case material from an ethnographic study of the process of assessment for older people, this research and subsequent papers examined what happens when practitioners try to understand the needs of individual older people through a process dominated by agency agendas. By marginalising the older person's insights, the risk of unwelcome or inappropriate intervention may increase. A user-centred approach, by contrast, requires information gathering and provision that is meaningful to the older person and sensitive to their efforts to analyse and manage their situation. These efforts are often revealed in narrative form as the person tells their story which, in an agency-centred assessment, is easily overlooked or even ignored. (Richards, 2000)

This research was undertaken before the concept of single assessment was being developed. The notion of a tension between meeting the needs of the agency and taking a user-centred approach warrants further consideration, as this is a balance that, as a practitioner working with older people, you will need to achieve.

The Department of Health circular (DoH, 2002b) which provides the initial guidance to agencies on the implementation of the single assessment process includes a number of annexes which give details on a range of 'implementation and practice matters', the first of which considers the 'key implications for older people'. Within this document, the Department of Health acknowledge that:

> Older people are the most important participants in the single assessment process. There are two reasons for this. First the assessment is about and for them. Second, of all the experts in the care of older people, the greatest experts are older people themselves. They will know when they are having difficulties, the nature of those difficulties, and what might be done to resolve them. In the past, assessments may have been done *to*, not *with*, older people; and services planned without considering their views and wishes. (DoH, 2002b)

Therefore this new assessment process should assist practitioners from all disciplines to take a user-centred approach when working with older people.

ACTIVITY 7.7

Reread the case study of Miss Shirley Bundle and Activity 7.6 where you considered the implications of the single assessment process for partnership working between agencies and professionals. Think about how you might feel if you were Shirley Bundle. How could the professionals working with you help you to meaningfully participate in the process and truly influence the decisions that are going to be made?

The case study and Figure 7.2 illustrating the potential numbers of people who may become involved in arranging or providing Miss Bundle's care show how the individual older person could be overwhelmed by the sheer number of different people they may meet. Given that Miss Bundle is experiencing pain and an increasing range of difficulties in her life, we could envisage that this influx of professionals could result in her feeling frightened, vulnerable and disempowered. The sheer balance of numbers between professionals and the service user and carer gives rise to an unequal distribution of power. That imbalance coupled with the professional roles and responsibilities assumed by the individuals involved, could further disadvantage and disempower Miss Bundle.

There are a number of ways in which this uneven balance of power could be partially addressed to ensure that Miss Bundle is able to participate in the assessment process meaningfully. Within the single assessment process domains, for example the first domain is 'User's perspective' and covers 'Problems and issues in the user's own words' and 'User's expectations and motivation'. Additionally, attention to the following areas through the assessment would enhance the older person's participation in the process;

- *Ensuring that the older person has relevant, timely and comprehensive information, provided in a format that they are able to understand*. This means that the social worker may need to provide information in verbal, written or diagrammatic formats, for example. It may be necessary to repeat some details or consider offering the same information in a number of ways, possibly sign language, Braille or large print, or different language materials could be appropriate. The worker will need to confirm the older person's understanding, as sharing information is a fundamental process if the service user is to be empowered. It is only with all the information available to them that an older person can make a meaningful contribution and realistic choices.

- *Ensuring that all aspects of the work with the older person are appropriate and timely.* As you have seen with the case study, it is possible that at the time of intervention of services, the service user is facing a crisis point in their lives and may be frightened and feel disempowered and vulnerable. It is crucial, therefore, that the social worker is sensitive to the needs of the older person and adjusts their contact with that person accordingly.

- *Listening to the older person and adopting the biographical approach.* By actively listening to the older person's own account and enabling them to influence the processes through prioritising what is important to that individual, the service will become user-centred.

- *Taking a strengths-based approach to assessment.* Parker and Bradley (2003) describe this approach as a mechanism for reducing the power imbalance in the service user/worker relationship. Taking an exchange model approach, the social worker facilitates 'service users to identify their needs and explore alternative ways of acting or conceptualising their experiences' (page 14). In this way, the service user is recognised as the expert in their own needs and their opinions, ideas and perspectives are valued and will influence the outcomes.

- *Self-assessment.* The National Service Framework for Older People states that elements of self-assessment should be considered within the overview assessment of the SAP (page 32). This would seem the logical development from the exchange model strengths-based approach described above.

- *Working with the older person to increase their autonomy and independence.* Social work practice through all the social work processes should aim to promote the older person's autonomy and independence. With this overarching aim to assessment and intervention the practitioner will be effectively passing some of their power to the service-user. One of the ways in which the older person can be enabled is through practice that supports the maintenance and development of formal and informal networks that meet the needs and wishes of the older person.

  By working with the service user to examine and consider support networks which they can access and develop, the social worker may enable the older person to increase the resources available to them to increase their independence, capacity and power to influence factors that affect their life.

The single assessment process domains include consideration of 'Relationships', in particular 'Social contacts, relationships and involvement' and 'Caring arrangements'. As you have seen in Chapter 3 of this book, there is both legislation and guidance that requires professionals to take account of the needs of informal carers. It is important that the skills and knowledge you employ when working in partnership with service users to meaningfully enable them to participate in their care arrangements are also used when working with carers. Each of the points discussed above equally apply to undertaking carer assessments and working with carers to support them in assessing, providing and making care arrangements for older people.

RESEARCH SUMMARY

The involvement of the user in the shaping of services is growing and there is a concern that people who use services seek not just to recount their experience, but to use it as a foundation for research, policy formation and the construction of theory.

The Centre for Citizen Participation, based at Brunel University, undertakes a number of user-controlled, emancipatory and user-led research projects. It is concerned both with supporting service user involvement in research and evaluation and on developing user-controlled and emancipatory research approaches. For example, it is concerned to develop a model of involvement for older people. (Based on: www.brunel.ac.uk/depts/health/research/ccp.htm)

'Shaping Our Lives' is a national independent users' network that aims to give users a stronger and more equal voice in defining outcomes in social care. Its aims are to support the development of local user involvement to deliver better outcomes for service users and to give a shared voice to user-controlled organisations.

The 'Shaping Our Lives' project, funded by the Joseph Rowntree Foundation, has been one initiative that has sought to take this agenda forward in terms of research, development projects and the formulation of ideas, perspectives and conclusions that arise out of service user experience (Turner et al., 2003; Turner, 2003). (Based on: www.shapingourlives.org.uk)

Peter Beresford is professor of a social policy and director of the Centre for Citizen Participation at Brunel Unversity, the chair of the national service user network 'Shaping Our Lives' and a long-term user of mental health services. Peter Beresford (2003) states that the closer you are to direct experience the more you know about that experience. He argues that user involvement in research should not be tokenistic and stresses the need for the systematic and coherent evaluation of such involvement in research.

C H A P T E R   S U M M A R Y

In this chapter you have examined the knowledge and skills required to develop social work practice with older people that ensures the meaningful participation of all stakeholders. In Chapter 3, you read about the single assessment process (SAP) from the National Service Framework for Older People (DoH, 2001a). Your knowledge of the SAP has been further developed in this chapter, as this framework has been used as an example through which to discuss the concepts of partnership and participation in practice.

In the first section of the chapter you were offered a number of terms related to partnership working and their definitions were considered. You were also given some of the historical context to the drives towards partnership working. Thereafter, you explored issues of partnership and participation from different levels, firstly considering the implications for working together at a structural and strategic level, then at the level of the agency, teams and individual professionals. Within these sections, you were offered different theories and research projects that attempt to explain the issues associated with working across professional boundaries.

Throughout the chapter we have argued that an approach that encompasses a range of professional perspectives should be developed, but more importantly an approach that puts the individual older person at its centre will enable an integrated approach with shared values and objectives. So, in the final section you examined how older people who use social work services and informal carers can be enabled to participate in assessment and service provision in ways that will increase their resources, capacity and power to influence factors that affect their lives.

Gubrium, J. and Holstein, J. (eds) (2003) *Ways of Aging*. Oxford: Blackwell

This book takes a biographical approach to exploring diversity in the experience of growing and being older. The editors present a compelling collection of ten original essays demonstrating the importance of giving older people a voice and, through this, understanding their unique and varied experiences.

Means, R., Richards, S. and Smith, R. (2003) *Community Care Policy and Practice*, 3rd edn. Basingstoke: Palgrave Macmillan.

This book has three chapters that are of particular relevance to the issues of partnership and participation, namely: Chapter 5 within which the authors debate developments and perspectives on joint working; Chapter 6 which looks specifically at housing and community care; and Chapter 7 which takes a critical perspective on issues of user empowerment.

www.integratedcarenetwork.gov.uk

The Integrated Care Network website aims to help frontline organisations to work together. The website is organised around key themes, and within each theme relevant research, discussion, debate and a resources database are provided.

Concluding remarks

This book has taken a distinctive focus on social work practice within the specific practice context of working with older people. As you have worked through the activities, research summaries and case studies you will have developed your knowledge, understanding and skills in respect of working with older people. Your developing understanding of work in this specific social work practice context will enable you to promote and protect the individual and collective well-being of older people with whom you work.

Throughout the book you have been encouraged to interact and engage with the information and the ideas that have been presented. You have considered a number of case studies and summaries of contemporary research that illustrate and draw out key points to reinforce your understanding and develop your skills of analysis and synthesis. At the end of each chapter you have been provided with suggestions for further reading, relevant Internet resources and current government guidance and policy documents, all of which evidence and support best social work practice when working with older people.

As a social worker working with older people you are in a privileged position. While there are many assumptions in society that suggest that older people are one homogenous group of people and that growing older holds a range of common expectations, in terms of life course development the reverse is actually true. You will be working with a diverse and varied group of people where it is possible that the only similarity between them is the effects of the disadvantage and stereotyping notions imposed by the social construction of old age. We are all aware that each one of us is growing older and that there are some expected biological and sociological transitions that may occur in that process. However, none of these changes are inevitable or fixed.

Throughout your studies of this book, you will have considered a perspective on growing older that values the richness of people's ageing experiences. We acknowledge that when working with older people, you may be working with people who are vulnerable, who are potentially oppressed and disadvantaged. However, we have stressed the significance of each individual's life experiences and the meanings that they attach to growing older in their own circumstances. Every older person that you work with brings a rich history of personal experiences and meanings to the working relationship that you develop with them. With this perspective, you have then been able to appreciate how best social work practice can empower and enable older people to raise their self-esteem, and take and maintain control of their lives.

Social work practice with older people is both challenging and rewarding. In each one of the practice situations where you are working with an older person, you should take account of the whole range of issues covered in the chapters of this book. For example, in your practice you need to demonstrate awareness of the legal and political context of your work (Chapter 3), coupled with an understanding of the experiences of that older person in their specific situation (Chapters 4 and 5). You also need to be alert to potentially abusive situations (Chapter 6), while developing practice that works in partnership with older people and other agencies (Chapter 7). Developing a holistic approach to your practice will assist you to take account of older people's situation in society and the values and ethics of social work practice with older people (Chapters 1 and 2).

We hope that as you have studied this book you will have been encouraged to reflect upon your developing knowledge and that you will take your studies further by exploring the recommended reading and Internet resources that have been suggested. You should spend a little time reflecting on the key themes of the book, your learning and how you might meet the six National Occupational Standards for social work and promote the values enshrined within the Code of Practice for social workers. This book can be used in a way that allows you to revisit aspects of social work practice with older people. Key Role 6 of the National Occupational Standards requires you to 'demonstrate professional competence in social work practice' through working within 'agreed standards of social work practice and ensuring your own professional development'. As a professional social worker you will continue to learn, develop your practice and update your knowledge and skills. Through reflection-upon-practice, reading and researching evidence of best practice, learning from peers and engaging in practice supervision you will ensure your continued professional development. The learning you have achieved from this text will contribute to your development as a skilled social worker who works effectively with older people and their carers. The ways you progress and develop your learning further will be, to some extent, unique to you.

References

Age Concern (2004) *Caring for Someone with Depression*. Powys: Age Concern.

Ahmad, W., Darr, A., Jones, L. and Nisar, G. (1998) *Deafness and Ethnicity: Services, Policy and Politics*. Bristol: Policy Press.

Ahmed, F. and Cheeseman, C. (1996) *Why Can't You See Me? A study into the needs of people with visual impairment from ethnic communities living in a London borough*. Available at: **www.seeability.org**.

Anttonen, A., Baldock, J. and Sipilä, J. (2003) *The Young, the Old and the State*. Cheltenham: Edward Elgar.

Audit Commission (1986) *Making a Reality of Community Care*. London: HMSO.

Audit Commission (1997) *The Coming of Age*. Available at: **www.audit-commission.gov.uk**.

Audit Commission (2002) *Integrated Services for Older People: Building a Whole System Approach in England*. Available at: **www.audit-commission.gov.uk**.

Audit Commission (2004a) *Older People – Building a Strategic Approach*. London: Audit Commission.

Audit Commission (2004b) *Support for Carers of Older People*. London: Audit Commission.

Baker, A. (1975) Granny bashing. *Modern Geriatrics*, 5(8): 20–4.

Banks, S. (2001) *Ethics and Values in Social Work*, 2nd edn. Basingstoke: Palgrave Macmillan.

Barnett, S. (2002) Deafblind culture in the UK. *Dbi Review*, Jan.–Jun.

Beresford, P. (2003) *It's Our Lives: A Short Theory of Knowledge, Distance and Experience*. London: Citizen Press.

Better Government for Older People (1999) *Making It Happen: Briefing 1*. Wolverhampton: BGOP.

Beveridge, W. (1942) *Social Insurance and Allied Services*. London: HMSO.

Biestek, F. (1961) *The Casework Relationship*. London: Allen & Unwin.

Biggs, S., Phillipson, C. and Kingston, P. (1995) *Elder Abuse in Perspective*. Buckingham: Open University Press.

Block, M. and Sinnott, I. (1979) *The Battered Elder Syndrome*. Georgetown, MD: University of Maryland Press.

Bond, J., Coleman, P. and Pearce, S. (eds) (1993) *Ageing in Society: Introduction to Social Gerontology*, 2nd edn. London: Sage.

Butler, R.N. and Lewis, M.I. (1973) *Aging and Mental Health*. St Louis, MD: C.V. Mosby.

Bytheway, B. (1995) *Ageism*. Buckingham: Open University Press.

Bytheway, B., Bacigaluo, V., Bornat, J., Johnson, J. and Spurr, S. (eds) (2002) *Understanding Care, Welfare and Community: A Reader*. London: Routledge.

Cabinet Office (1999) *Modernising Government*. London: Stationery Office.

Community Care (2004) Call to extend remit of Valuing People. *Community Care*, May, 20–6. Available at: **www.communitycare.co.uk**.

Crawford, K. and Walker, J. (2003) *Social Work and Human Development*. Exeter: Learning Matters.

Department of Health (1989) *Caring for People: Community Care in the Next Decade and Beyond*. London: HMSO.

Department of Health (1990a) *Care Management and Assessment: Managers' Guide*. London: HMSO.

Department of Health (1990b) *Community Care in the Next Decade and Beyond: Policy Guidance*. London: HMSO.

Department of Health (1991) *Care Management and Assessment: Practitioners' Guide*. London: HMSO.

Department of Health (1992) *Confronting Elder Abuse*. London: HMSO.

Department of Health (1997a) *Who Decides?* London: HMSO.

Department of Health (1997b) *The New NHS: Modern, Dependable*. London: Stationery Office.

Department of Health (1998a) *Modernising Social Services: Partnership in Action*. London: HMSO.

Department of Health (1998b) *Modernising Social Services: Promoting Independence, Improving Protection, Raising Standards*. London: Stationery Office.

Department of Health (1999a) *The National Service Framework for Mental Health*. London: Stationery Office.

Department of Health (1999b) *Caring about Carers: A National Strategy for Carers*. London: DoH.

Department of Health (2000a) No Secrets: *Guidance on Developing and Implementing Multi-agency Policies and Procedures to Protect Vulnerable Adults from Abuse*, DoH Circular HSC 2000/007. Available at: **www.doh.gov.uk/scg/nosecrets.htm**.

Department of Health (2000b) *Community Care (Direct Payments) Act 1996: Policy and Practice Guidance*, 2nd edn. London: DoH.

Department of Health (2000c) *A Quality Strategy for Social Care*. London: DoH.

Department of Health (2000d) *The NHS Plan: A Plan for Investment, a Plan for Reform*. London: Stationery Office.

Department of Health (2001a) *The National Service Framework for Older People*. London: Stationery Office. Available at: **www.doh.gov.uk/nsf/olderpeople.htm**.

Department of Health (2001b) *Valuing People: A New Strategy for Learning Disability for the 21st Century*. London: Stationery Office.

Department of Health (2001c) *Continuing Care: NHS and Local Councils' Responsibilities*, HSC 2001/015, LAC(2001)18. London: Stationery Office.

Department of Health (2002a) *Fair Access to Care Services: Guidance on Eligibility Criteria for Adult Social Care,* LAC (2002) 13. London: Stationery Office.

Department of Health (2002b) *The Single Assessment Process Guidance for Local Implementation.* Available at: **www.doh.gov.uk/scg/sap/locimp.htm**.

Department of Health (2002c) *Guidance on the Single Assessment Process for Older People,* HSC 2002/001; LAC (2002) 1. Available at: **www.doh.gov.uk/publications.coinh.html**.

Department of Health (2002d) *The NHS Plan.* London: Stationery Office.

Department of Health (2003) *The Community Care, Services for Carers and Children's Services* (Direct Payments) Guidance. London: HMSO.

Department of Health (2004) *Policy Guidance – Identification and Notification of Sight Loss.* Available at: **www.dh.gov.uk**.

Deputy Prime Minister (1998) *Modern Local Government: In Touch with the People* London: Stationery Office.

Dominelli, L. (2002) Values in social work: contested entities with enduring qualities. In R. Adams, L. Dominelli and M. Payne (eds), *Critical Practice in Social Work.* Basingstoke: Palgrave Macmillan.

Douglass, R., Hickey, T. and Noel, C. (1980) *A Study of Maltreatment of the Elderly and Other Vulnerable Adults.* Ann Arbor, MI: University of Michigan Press.

Eastman, M. (1984) *Old Age Abuse.* Mitchum: Age Concern.

Eastman, M. (1988) Granny abuse. *Community Outlook,* October: 15–16.

Eastman, M. and Sutton, M. (1982) Granny bashing. *Geriatric Medicine,* November: 11–15.

Erikson, E. (1995) *Childhood and Society.* London: Vintage.

Esping-Andersen, G. (1996) *Welfare States in Transition.* London: Sage.

Felson, D.T., Anderson, J.J. and Hannan, M.T. (1989) Impaired vision and hip fractures: The Framington Study. *Journal of American Geriatric Society,* 37: 495–500.

Foote, C. and Stanners, C. (2002) *Integrated Care for Older People.* London: Jessica Kingsley.

Fulmer, T. and O'Malley, T. (1987) *Inadequate Care of the Elderly.* New York: Springer.

General Social Care Council (GSCC) (2002) *Codes of Practice for Social Care Workers and Employers.* London: GSCC.

Glasby, J. and Littlechild, R (2002) *Social Work and Direct Payments.* Bristol: Policy Press.

Glasby, J. and Littlechild, R. (2004) *The Health and Social Care Divide: The Experiences of Older People.* Bristol: Policy Press.

Golightley, M. (2004) *Social Work and Mental Health. Exeter:* Learning Matters.

Graham, H. (2000) Applying a community needs profiling approach to tackling service user poverty. *British Journal of Social Work,* 30: 3.

Griffiths, R. (1988) *Community Care: Agenda for Action.* London: HMSO.

Gubrium, J. and Holstein, J. (eds) (2003) *Ways of Aging.* Oxford: Blackwell.

Hetherington, R. (2001) The educational opportunities for cross-national comparisons. *Social Work in Europe*, 3(1).

Hockey, J. and James, A. (2003) *Social Identities across the Life Course.* Basingstoke: Palgrave Macmillan.

Hocking, D. (1988) Miscare – a form of abuse in the elderly. *Update*, 15 May: 2411–19.

Hogg, J. and Lambe, L. (1998) *Older People with Learning Disabilities: A Review of the Literature on Residential Services and Family Caregiving.* The Foundation for People with Learning Disabilities, available at: **www.learningdisabilities.org.uk**.

Holland, A.J., Hon, J., Huppert, F.A., Stevens, F. and Watson, P. (1998) Population-based study of the prevalence and presentation of dementia in adults with Down's syndrome. *British Journal of Psychiatry*, 172: 493–8.

Home Office (1998) *Speaking up for Justice.* London: HMSO.

Home Office (1999) *Action for Justice.* London: HMSO.

Hopkins, G. (2003) Barrier busters. *Community Care Magazine*, 2–8 October; available at: **www.community-care.co.uk**.

House of Commons Health Committee (1995) Long-term Care: NHS *Responsibilities for Meeting Continuing Health Care Needs*, HSG(95)8. London: HMSO.

Housing Corporation (2002) *Housing for Older People: The Corporation's housing policy for older people*. Available at: **www.housingcorplibrary.org.uk**.

Housing Corporation (2003) *Strategy for Housing Older People in England: The Housing Corporation's new strategy for housing older people*. Available at **www.housingcorplibrary.org.uk**.

Howe, D. (2002) Relating theory to practice. In M. Davies (ed.), *The Blackwell Companion to Social Work,* 2nd edn. Oxford: Blackwell.

Hughes, B. (1995) *Older People and Community Care: Critical Theory and Practice.* Buckingham: Open University Press.

Hughes, A. (2001) Comment on No Secrets. In J. Pritchard (ed.), *Good Practice with Vulnerable Adults*. London: Jessica Kingsley.

Hughes, B. and Mtezuka, E.M. (1992) Social work and older women. In M. Langan and L. Day (eds), *Women, Oppression and Social Work: Issues in Anti-discriminatory Practice*. London: Routledge.

Hugman, R. (1994) *Ageing and the Care of Older People in Europe*. Basingstoke: Macmillan.

Johns, R. (2003) *Using the Law in Social Work.* Exeter: Learning Matters.

Johns, R. and Sedgwick, A. (1999) *Law for Social Work Practice: Working with Vulnerable Adults*. Basingstoke: Macmillan.

Kitwood, T. (1990) The dialectics of dementia: with particular reference to Alzheimer's disease. *Ageing and Society*, 10(2): 177–96.

Kitwood, T. (1993) Frames of reference for an understanding of dementia. In J. Johnson and R. Slater (eds), *Ageing and Later Life*. London: Sage.

Kitwood, T. (2002) Malignant social psychology. In B. Bytheway, V. Bacigalupo, J. Bornat, J. Johnson and S. Spurr (eds), *Understanding Care, Welfare and Community: A Reader*. London: Routledge.

Koprowska, J. (forthcoming) *Communication and Interpersonal Skills in Social Work*. Exeter: Learning Matters.

Kurrle, S. (2001) The role of the medical practitioner. In J. Pritchard (ed.), *Good Practice with Vulnerable Adults*. London: Jessica Kingsley.

Lewis, J. (2002) The boundary between health and social care for older people. In B. Bytheway, V., Bacigalupo, J., Bornat, J., Johnson and S. Spurr (eds), *Understanding Care, Welfare and Community: A Reader*. London: Routledge.

Local Government Association (LGA) (2003) *All Our Tomorrows – Inverting the Triangle of Care*. ADSS. Available at: **www.adss.org.uk**.

Lorenze, W. (1994) *Social Work in Changing Europe*. London: Routledge.

Lovelock, R. and Powell, J. with Craggs, S. (1995) *Assessing the Social Support Needs of Visually Impaired People*. York: Joseph Rowntree Foundation.

Loxley, A. (1997) *Collaboration in Health and Welfare: Working with Difference*. London: Jessica Kingsley.

McDonald, A. (1999) *Understanding Community Care*. Basingstoke: Palgrave Macmillan.

Malin, N., Manthorpe, J., Rose, D. and Wilmot, S. (1999) *Community Care for Nurses and the Caring Professions*. Buckingham: Open University Press.

Mansell, J.L. (1993) *Services for People with Learning Disabilities: Challenging Behaviour or Mental Health Needs*. Project Group Report, Mind.

Marks, D. (1999) *Disability: Conversational Debates and Psychological Perspectives*. London: Routledge.

Means, R., Morbey, H. and Smith, R. (2002) *From Community Care to Market Care?* Bristol: Policy Press.

Means, R., Richards, S. and Smith, R. (2003) *Community Care Policy and Practice*. Basingstoke: Palgrave Macmillan.

Mind (2004) *Mental Health Problems and Learning Disabilities*. Information factsheet available from: **www.mind.org.uk/information/facts**.

MORI (2001) *Grey Power and Class Voting*. Available at: **www.mori.com**.

Morris, J. (1997) *Community Care: Working in Partnership with Service Users*. Birmingham: Venture Press.

Mullender, A. (2002) Gendering the social work agenda. In M. Davies (ed.), *The Blackwell Companion to Social Work*. Oxford: Blackwell.

Nilsson, M., Ekman, S. and Sarvimaki, A. (1998) Ageing with joy or resigned to older age: older people's experiences of the quality of life in older age. *Health Care in Later Life*, 3(2): 94–110.

Nolan, M.R. (1997) *Health and Social Care: What the Future Holds for Nursing.* Keynote address at the Third Royal College of Nursing of Older People European Conference and Exhibition, Harrogate.

Norman, A. (1985) *Triple Jeopardy: Growing Old in a Second Homeland.* London: Centre for Policy on Ageing.

Nuffield Centre for Community Care Studies (2000) *Integration of Health and Social Services Provision.* Available at: **www.gla.ac.uk/centres/nuffield/**.

Office for National Statistics (1999) *Social Focus on Older People.* London: Stationery Office.

Oliver, M. (1996) *Understanding Disability: From Theory to Practice.* Basingstoke: Macmillan.

O'Malley, H., Segel, H. and Perez, R. (1979) *Elder Abuse in Massachusetts.* Boston, MA: Legal Research and Services to the Elderly.

Parker, J. and Bradley, G. (2003) *Social Work Practice: Assessment, Planning, Intervention and Review.* Exeter: Learning Matters.

Pritchard, J. (1995) *The Abuse of Older People,* 2nd edn. London: Jessica Kingsley.

Pritchard, J. (ed.) (2001a) *Good Practice with Vulnerable Adults.* London: Jessica Kingsley.

Pritchard, J. (2001b) *Male Victims of Elder Abuse: Their Experiences and Needs.* London: Jessica Kingsley.

Race, D. (ed.) (2002) *Learning Disability – A Social Approach.* London: Routledge.

Richards, S. (2000) Bridging the divide: elders and the assessment process. *British Journal of Social Work,* 30: 37–49.

RNIB (1997) *Losing Sight of Blindness.* London: RNIB.

RNIB (2003) *See Change.* London: RNIB.

Rowntree, B.S. (1901) *Poverty: A Study of Town Life.* London: Macmillan.

Ruth, J.E. and Oberg, P. (1996) Ways of life: old age in a life history perspective. In J.E. Birren, G.M. Kenyon, J.E. Schroots and T. Svensomm (eds), *Ageing and Biography: Explorations in Adult Development.* New York: Springer.

Ryan, T. (2001) Abuse issues relating to people with mental health problems. In J. Pritchard (ed.), *Good Practice with Vulnerable Adults.* London: Jessica Kingsley.

Schuman, J. (1999) The ethnic minority populations of Great Britain – latest estimates. *Population Trends,* Summer, 96: 33–43.

SCIE (2004) *Practice Guide: Assessing Mental Health Needs of Older People.* Available at: **www.scie.org.uk.**

Seebohm, F. (1968) *Report of the Committee on Local Authorities and Allied Personal Services,* Cmnd 3703. London: HMSO.

Smale, G. and Tuson, G. with Biehal, N. and Marsh, P. (1993) *Empowerment, Assessment, Care Management and the Skilled Worker.* London: NISW/HMSO.

Sontag, S. (1978) The double standard of ageing. In V. Carver and P. Liddiard (eds), *An Ageing Population.* Sevenoaks: Hodder & Stoughton.

Statham, D. (ed.) (2004) *Managing Front Line Practice in Social Care*. London: Jessica Kingsley.

Steverink, N., Lindeiberg, S. and Ornel, J. (1998) Towards understanding successful ageing: patterned changes in resources and goals. *Ageing and Society*, 18(4): 441–68.

Sugarman, L. (1986) *Life Span Development Concepts, Theories and Interventions.* London: Routledge.

Sumner, K (2002) *No Secrets The Protection of Vulnerable Adults from Abuse: Local Codes of Practice Findings from an Analysis of Local Codes of Practice.* London: Centre for Policy on Ageing. Available at: **www.cpa.org**.

Thompson, N. (2001) *Anti-Discriminatory Practice*, 3rd edn. Basingstoke: Palgrave Macmillan.

Thompson, N. (2002) Anti-discriminatory practice. In M. Davies (ed.), *The Blackwell Companion to Social Work*, 2nd edn. Oxford: Blackwell.

Thompson, N. (2003) *Promoting Equality,* 2nd edn. Basingstoke: Palgrave Macmillan.

Tinker, A. (1996) *Older People in Modern Society*, 4th edn. Harlow: Addison Wesley.

Townsend, P. (1962) *The Last Refuge.* London: Routledge & Kegan Paul.

Tregaskis, C. (2002) Social model theory: the story so far. *Disability and Society,* 17(4): 457–70.

Turk, V., Dodd, K. and Christmas, M. (2001) *Down's Syndrome and Dementia: Briefing for Commissioners*. London: Foundation for People with Learning Disabilities.

Turner M. (2003) *Our Lives – From Outset to Outcomes: What People Think of the Social Care Services They Use*. York: Joseph Rowntree Foundation.

Turner M., Brough, P. and William Finlay R.B. (2003) *Our Voice in Our Future: Service Users Debate the Future of the Welfare State*. York: Joseph Rowntree Foundation.

Union of Physical Impaired Against Segregation (1976) *Fundamental Principles of Disability.* London: UPIAS.

Vale, D. and Smythe, C. (2002) *Changing the Way We Think about Blindness: Myths and Realities.* London: RNIB.

Vernon, A. (2002) Multiple oppression and the disabled people's movement. In B. Bytheway, V. Bacigalupo, J. Bornat, J. Johnson and S. Spurr (eds), *Understanding Care, Welfare and Community: A Reader*. London: Routledge.

Victor, C. (1997) *Community Care and Older People*. Cheltenham: Stanley Thornes.

Wolfensberger, W. and Tullman, S. (2002) Community and stigma: the principle of normalization. In B. Bytheway, V. Bacigalupo, J. Bornat, J. Johnson and S. Spurr (eds), *Understanding Care, Welfare and Community: A Reader.* London: Routledge.

Index